BEYOND BELIEF

Also by Peter Spink

A Christian In The New Age
The End Of An Age
No Place To Hide
The Universal Christ
The Sevenfold Call
A Time For Knowledge

BEYOND BELIEF

How to develop mystical consciousness and discover the God within

PETER SPINK

PIATKUS

© 1996 Peter Spink

First published in 1996 by
Judy Piatkus (Publishers) Ltd
5 Windmill Street, London W1P 1HF

The moral right of the author has been asserted

A catalogue record for this book is
available from the British Library

ISBN 0–7499–1660–5

Edited by Carol Gardiner
Designed by Sue Ryall

Set in Bembo by
Phoenix Photosetting, Chatham, Kent
Printed and bound in Great Britain by
Mackays of Chatham PLC, Chatham, Kent

For Jim and Claire and all 'the People of the Way'

Acknowledgements

With gratitude to Winifred and Mollie for wrestling with the text and to Joan and Norman for giving me space. And in appreciation of Caroline Dorling who encouraged me to write the book.

Contents

1

Finding the God Within

God is neither perceptible to our senses
Nor conceived by our intellects
But He is sensible to the heart.

DIONYSIUS THE MYSTIC

'Excuse me, sir, could you please explain to me how I can find God?' The sudden and suprising request came from a hitch-hiker sitting in the back of my car. He was about thirty years of age and for half an hour he had been listening intently to the conversation between my other three passengers on the theme of the weekend retreat to which we were travelling – 'The God Within'.

'For many years,' he continued, 'I have wanted to believe in a God, but I am repelled by the only one I hear about: the God of the boxes.' He went on to explain that by 'boxes' he meant competing belief systems. 'I am still looking for the God of *experience*.'

Beyond Belief is for all those who, like the hitch-hiker, are looking for a God who cannot be encapsulated into any one creed, who can be known and experienced directly. Written in the form of a journey, my hope is that it will guide you to a dimension within yourself where such a God is to be found.

You may wonder how you can recognise this dimension. Its

characteristics are twofold. Firstly it reflects your deepest (i.e. authentic) need, and secondly it offers fulfilment of that need. Such need is beyond that of physical, mental and emotional fulfilment or material success. Paradoxically, it is fulfilment in these very areas which may cause you to recognise a previously unacknowledged need and hitherto untapped potential.

No prior beliefs are required for this journey. All that you need is a willingness to test the waters for yourself. Such testing needs to go beyond intellectual inquiry or curiosity and in this book, therefore, you are invited to experience the testing stage-by-stage and to allow experience to precede explanation. For the Western mind this is a reversal of the natural order of things and you will therefore need to exercise a measure of trust as you 'test' the experiential sections at the end of each chapter.

There is a story about the famous acrobat, Blondin. On one occasion he was about to demonstrate his skill not only by walking upon but by pushing a wheelbarrow along a tightrope when he noticed a small boy watching him intently. Turning to the boy he asked, 'Do you believe that I can push this wheelbarrow along the rope?' Promptly the boy replied, 'Yes, sir.' Blondin enquired further, 'Do you believe I could safely do that with a small boy in the wheelbarrow?' Again came the ready response, 'Yes, sir.' 'Then will you trust me to take you in the wheelbarrow?' 'No, thank you very much, sir.'

Belief does not necessarily imply commitment, trust does. The journey offered by *Beyond Belief* invites you both to acknowledge and to trust in your own Divine potential. And the invitation is open both to those whose spiritual search operates independently of religious structures and frameworks and also to those who, nurtured within a religious context and thankful for the light which that nurture has shown on their path so far, are seeking to widen their horizons to a full recognition of a God who indwells all Creation and who cannot be confined within human structures.

Bigotry and obscurantism of any kind is totally alien to an

authentic spiritual path. This does not mean lack of discernment. Rather the reverse is true. I suggest you read each chapter slowly and practise the exercises and meditations in the form they are given so you will learn to see with the eyes of the heart where the capacity for non-judgemental discrimination lies. Learn to see before asking the question 'What is seeing?'

The guidelines and signposts offered on this journey stem largely from my own spiritual journey over many years. As a teenager the journey began with a dramatic leap into a 'box' which quickly proved to be exclusive and excluding.

At the age of seventeen I had with all the intensity of adolescent fervour been drawn to the figure of Jesus Christ as portrayed in the Christian Scriptures and mirrored in the lives of some of my contemporaries. I was quickly absorbed and encased within the confines of a branch of the Christian Church whose interpretation of what constituted allegiance to Christ silenced and suffocated all enquiry. A great deal of struggle involving both pain and joy led me eventually to an equally decisive exit from the box and I caught glimpses of the Cosmic or universal Christ towards which Jesus so clearly points. Undreamed-of vistas of possibility and ever-widening horizons unfolded before me. My hope is that this book will lead you too towards these horizons.

Beginning the journey

In *Beyond Belief* I begin the journey with a panoramic view of human concepts of Divinity throughout history. It will pose two questions. Is God Him or Herself evolving in and through Creation, and is a fully-realised humanity also an experience of the God reality?

The journey proceeds through the stage-by-stage cultivation of your faculty for direct knowledge. For this reason it is important not to regard *Beyond Belief* as a textbook of questions and answers. More questions are raised than answers given. The very *raison d'être* of the journey you are taking is to learn the art of answering your own questions as they relate to your own experience of life.

An awakened heart leads to an entirely new way of looking at life, yourself, others, contemporary society and ultimately at the whole created order. For the Cosmos is also on a journey. What this means in practical and everyday terms will differ for each of us. The meditative exercises are designed not only to assist and encourage self-realisation but also to encourage an understanding of how evolving human beings relate to an evolving universe.

Food for the soul

It is my experience that serious and profound truths are often illuminated by humour and I have not hesitated to use it in this book. What has been called the 'medicine of immortality' or 'food for the soul' often becomes more palatable and better digested when accompanied by a dose of humour. Often in my work I have found that the bitter and the sweet closely accompany one another.

Early in my ministry as a priest I was literally shaken into a realisation of this. It fell to my lot to preside at a funeral. The day was wet and windy and the ground surrounding the freshly dug grave was sodden and crumbling. The coffin containing a much loved and deeply mourned local lady was lowered and I stepped foward to perform the last rites. I took one step too far, the earth gave way, and I was catapulted into the grave. There was a stunned silence broken by a voice from the rear of the group of mourners: 'Are you going with her, Father?' Tears of grief suddenly gave way to hysterical laughter as I was hauled to safety.

Sadness, suffering, pain and joy are all part of the human lot. The spiritual path provides no escape from life's perturbations but it will offer you a way of integrating life's contradictions into a positive whole.

A map for your journey

For the purpose of our journey we shall need a simple working definition or 'map' of the human being. For the purpose of moving 'beyond belief' into direct knowledge I propose a very simple definition: human beings are composed of body, emotions, intellect and beyond these three a spiritual potential. This potential, when awakened and nurtured, permeates and brings into a harmonious whole all the other parts, thus effecting a union of humanity and divinity.

Beyond Belief has two underlying assumptions. The first is that if you have a desire to discern and relate to the full potential within yourself, a potential which I call the 'God dimension', then this is possible now. This was described to me in my youth as 'a law of life' by a wise old farmer, known locally as 'a man of God'. 'If,' he assured me, 'you have a genuine desire to know your true self then be sure that you will. For that very desire comes from what we know as "God", and He cannot be denied.'

The second assumption is that crossing the barriers separating the conflicting belief systems there is a universal experience of God. The validity of this experience is attested not by commitment to particular dogmas, but rather by the evidence of a fully integrated life. This common experience may be interpreted in various different ways.

This is beautifully illustrated in the Indian story of the four friends who stumbled across an elephant in the dark. Unable to see the animal they each explored its contours with their hands. The first discovered the four legs. 'Here,' he cried, 'are the columns of a great temple.' The second felt the animal's powerful flanks. 'We have surely come upon a massive fortress,' he exclaimed, whilst the third tugged upon the tail which he declared to be a bellrope. The fourth discovered the trunk. 'There,' he assured his companions, 'is a huge serpent with some mystical significance.' Each had discovered and in some way experienced the reality of touching the elephant. Each interpreted the experience in his own way. No one explanation was complete in itself.

There is another important aspect to this story. The four friends explored the phenomenon with their hands. With the benefit of light and the faculty of sight they would have perceived the reality quite differently. None of the four would have claimed exclusive possession of the truth, nor could they have boxed in their definition of what they had encountered.

As far as possible, in describing this journey of exploration, I have tried to avoid what I regard as overworked religious words. For many of us such words carry with them powerful connotations of the 'gods of the boxes'. The essence of such words as 'salvation', 'enlightenment' and the more modern 'wholeness' may be fully comprehended by reference to a 'fully integrated life'. Such integration is best articulated not by the language of religion but by the evidence of the universally acknowledged witness of love, joy, peace, gentleness, patience and humility. These, not religious beliefs, validate a life. These do no less than constitute the very nature of God.

Awakening the heart

As you have seen, fundamental to the journey you are about to take is the awakening and employment of your faculty for direct or intuitive knowledge, a capacity latent within each one of us. I use the word 'latent', for in the Western world neither secular nor religious systems of education recognise and develop this fundamentally important aspect of the human mind. Because of this, the faculty lies dormant beneath the level of the conscious mind. When awakened we develop sight beyond that of sensual perception. A capacity to see beyond the apparent is brought into operation. A great spiritual master of the first century AD, Paul of Tarsus, wrote a letter to his disciples: 'I pray that the eyes of your heart may be opened, that you may KNOW . . .' (Letter to the Ephesians 3).

I recall a vivid example of such an awakening whilst exercising pastoral responsibility for one of England's great cathedrals. It was customary once a year for the eight weeks prior to Easter to recommend a book for study and reflection. With some temerity I had recommended the *Phenomenon of Man* by Father Pierre Teilhard de Chardin, a scientist, mystic and scholar. In his introduction to the book Sir Julian Huxley gives a summary as follows:

> *The* Phenomenon of Man *is a very remarkable book by a very remarkable man. In it the author has effected a threefold synthesis of the material and physical world with the world of mind and spirit: of the past with the future.*

The systematic study of such a book might be expected to present a daunting task to all but those with some scientific training. At the end of the allotted period I enquired cautiously of one reader, a lady of no special ability or training. 'How did you like the book?' She replied at once with enthusiasm, 'Intellectually much of it was quite beyond me, and as for "study and reflection" I don't think I got very far, for it was difficult to grasp with my head, but I knew that beyond the words was a reality with which I completely resonated in my heart. Somehow I knew that I was in touch with something quite wonderful, something which I find quite difficult to put into words.' She continued, 'I long to understand and to develop this knowledge.'

Mystical consciousness and discernment

The path you will follow in this book may be described as that of 'the journey inward'. In a book to which he gave this title, *The Journey Inward* (Darton, Longman and Todd, 1968), F. C. Happold writes:

An old age is dying, and a new age is being painfully born. It is characterised by a shaking of the foundations of religious faith . . . yet within this materialistic and secular civilisation there is a vast discontent . . . and an ardent desire for some sort of inner vision which will show the way to That we call God.

Today's great discovery for many on a spiritual search is that in the context of the shaking of the foundations, old images of remote and capricious gods are toppling and giving way to one who is within us and who cries out for recognition.

Such recognition is the first and decisive step on an exciting journey through the door of 'the opened heart' into 'mystical consciousness'. This raises questions such as 'How does this relate to religion? Are the two incompatible or can they coexist and does mysticism have a life of its own?' We will examine these issues later in the book.

Opening yourself to, and cultivation of, mystical consciousness requires the practice of 'the presence of God'. The meditation exercises will guide you step-by-step in this process.

A pitfall to be avoided in the journey is what has been called the process of 'ever learning yet never coming to a knowledge of the truth'. Because we in the West are conditioned to equate learning with acquiring information, you will be helped to distinguish between the two.

It has also been my experience that nothing provides a more effective escape from the exercise of discernment and the capacity to distinguish between the real and the unreal than the use of religious jargon. That the definition of a reality is not to be confused with the ability itself might be thought to be self-evident. For those bred and nurtured within a particular ecclesiastical tradition, this is far from the case.

No part of our humanity is to be negated nor rejected. For this reason self-acceptance should underline your approach to the journey. The traditional distinction between body and spirit is, I believe, misleading in that it supposes a dichotomy between matter and energy, between the material and the spiritual. For too long this has given rise to the false notion that body and spirit are opposed to each other, the former being a hindrance to the latter.

There is at the heart of the human being that which I have called the essence or impulse for life in all its aspects. This essence manifests itself in and through the physical, mental and emotional bodies. It permeates the whole and is always seeking to draw the integrated human being into union with the Source of all things. The manner of its expression is determined by the will or selfhood (ego).

As for the pilgrim in John Bunyan's *Pilgrim's Progress*, there are bypath meadows and pitfalls of illusion and delusion to be avoided. We will examine these in Chapter 9. You will be helped to cultivate a capacity for discernment, and so move forward with assurance.

A pathway to fulfilment

I have said little explicitly about sin. Beyond the statement that sin is separation from God, everything that could be said has been repeated so often that to delineate it further simply reduces its impact. Rather I have implied, I hope consistently, the need to give ourselves constantly to the release of our God-given potential, without which we are nothing.

Does the journey of discovery lead to sheltered seclusion and escape from the 'storms of life'? By no means. What I want to offer with confidence is a pathway leading to a full and fulfilled life, and an assurance of being part of a plan and purpose embracing life in all its dimensions, and the planet itself.

Beyond Belief offers guidelines and clues leading to knowledge which you already have, to perceptions which lie just below the surface of your mind, waiting to emerge. All discoveries which are authentic will not only clearly present themselves as 'your truth', they will also have universal implications.

Each one of us must discover these truths for ourselves as we follow the meditational guidelines and test the clues.

In my teens, I had a Biblical Promise Box. In this box tightly packed together there were about fifty Biblical texts. To read one it was necessary to carefully unroll the scroll. For the purpose of the 'lucky dip' a small pair of forceps was provided. The accompanying instructions advised extracting a single scroll in 'your hour of need'. As an adolescent most of my hours could be described that way! I can look back now with some amusement and a little scepticism at this method of problem-solving. Yet I do not doubt that for many people the promise box was and probably still is a means of touching the real.

For most of the time and for most of us, life's problems are, at best, challenges to be worked through and perhaps, at worst, burdens we learn to bear. Rarely do answers come easily and there are few who do not have to live with some unsolved enigmas. What can be asserted with confidence is that, using all our God-given faculties and refusing to operate in solitude, there is for each one of us not only a way of coping but a path of fulfilment.

Expectations on the journey

At what level, you may ask, should I pitch my expectations on this journey?

The wise, and indeed the wily, will view the path ahead as a *via media*, the middle way between extremes of self discipline and asceticism on the one hand and perpetual pandering to personal desire on the other. The expectancy, indeed confidence of achievement, will travel hand-in-hand with recognition that human frailty is our common lot, and from time to time this will be uppermost in our consciousness and experience. It has been said, perhaps tritely but nevertheless with truth, that 'to fall provides the opportunity for getting up'. Seen in this way we may find many unexpected opportunities for achievement!

Rose Macaulay, a mystic and author of the book *The Towers of Trebizond* (Fontana, 1990), describes how she was approached by a brash evangelist with the challenge 'Have you decided for Christ?' 'Yes,' she replied, 'many times, but always in a High Church, and it doesn't usually last very long.' The God we are seeking to realise is the God who comes to us along the lines with which we are familiar, so he is recognisable. The symbols of deity, religious or secular, which are real to me regardless of what speaks to another, are my symbols and for me it has always been a comfort to believe that 'God can write straight on the crooked lines of my life'.

The meditation exercises

To make sure that the reading of this book becomes more of a real experience for you, I have concluded each chapter with a meditational exercise. These meditations are directed towards centring in the heart. The basic pattern of the meditation will be built up stage by stage, as you work through the book. I have also provided a basic meditational guide in the Appendix which you may find it useful to refer to.

2

An Evolving God

*Is it possible to say with meaning that not only is man sub-
ject to the law of evolution, but so also in a particular way is
God? To some the question may sound blasphemous; it
has, however, been asked and is still being asked . . . .*

*Does God stand over against the universe or is He (or It)
also within? If we are prepared to say with the Hindu that
there is nothing which is not spirit . . . then in so far as
spirit and matter cohere within our space time continuum
. . . God may have to be said to evolve.*

F.C. HAPPOLD, *Religious Faith and Twentieth Century
Man* (Darton, Longman and Todd, 1980)

Standing on the threshold of the 'journey inward' you are on
the brink of an exploration and an adventure which without
doubt is also an exploration into God. Both patience and
expectation are fundamental to your journey. Expect to grow
stage by stage in understanding; be patient for explanations.
Each stage is important. From time to time you will look back
and say 'this is that' or in other words 'I now understand what I
have already experienced'.

You are about to follow a pathway which is intensely personal, for it begins where you are. All your individual life experiences are involved in the steps you are taking. Many of these
experiences have created within you the desire to move in this
direction. Yet, personal as the journey is to you, it has also a
universal dimension. For it is part of the great search which has
characterised the race since the dawn of human self-

consciousness. And to understand your personal path more clearly, it needs to be related to past and present shifts in human God-consciousness.

During the decade of the 1970s, I had become increasingly aware that some subtle yet definite change was taking place within the Western religious world of faith and practice. Forms of worship and religious ceremonies which had developed through many centuries, directed to a God 'out there', were giving way to simpler, less structured forms. Ritual was surrendering to spontaneity, the focus of attention was that of the human being rather than a 'Creator God' somewhere in outer space. The keynote of this change was the immanence of God that is 'the God within'. As I perceived it, devotionalism was giving way to interior awareness.

As a corollary to this change was evidence of a new approach to a spiritual path or commitment. Until recent times in the churches a valid 'interior' awareness was thought to be a rare experience reserved for an elitist body who had achieved this elevated state by passing through prescribed stages of preparation. Spirituality for ordinary believers had centred in faith rather than knowledge.

Yet Christendom, the predominant religion of the Western world and the religious tradition in which I had been nurtured, had always contained within itself seekers after interior awareness. Corporately the Quakers and individually a long line of outstanding mystics had followed this path. What impressed me as new was the widespread eruption of this awareness both within the ancient forms of worship and also outside of the ecclesiastical structures. This was no reformation of externals, but rather 'new wine appearing within old skins' on the one hand and on the other new spiritual movements quite independent of the old forms. It was as if some powerful magnetic attraction was drawing people together from a great diversity of backgrounds to a central point of consciousness.

Such people felt themselves to be part of a common intuitive quest, a search not for intellectual stimulus but for inner stillness and interior awareness. A new convergence was taking place.

I recall visiting a convent where the life of the nuns was ordered by strict and traditional rule. At the request of the Mother Superior I met with one of the nuns who had what she described to me as a 'theological problem'. 'You see, Father,' she explained, 'I have been given permission to lead a weekly meditation group. I give some guidance in techniques of relaxation and centring. Most of the one hour we then spend in silence. At the close, we articulate any thoughts we may wish to share.' It was during this time of sharing that the 'problem' had surfaced, for it was then that the startled Sister had discovered there were 'outsiders' in the group, that is, people with a different religious faith than that of the nuns, and others with no religious faith at all. 'My difficulty,' said the puzzled nun, 'is that until we start sharing concepts and ideas we all feel ourselves to be deeply at one in what we are doing and moving in the same direction.'

The event had raised in the Sister's mind a crucial question: How important in relation to human transformation is correct belief? I had long wrestled with this problem and had reached the conviction that only in so far as beliefs effected and with integrity represented the awakened heart have they any significance.

It was soon after this that with considerable excitement I came across the following words by F.C. Happold in a book first published just after the Second World War, 'Religious Faith and Twentieth Century Man (Darton, Longman and Todd, new edn. 1980): 'It is likely that towards the end of this century the only religion acceptable to Western Man will be a mystical one, mystical in terms of experiential wisdom.'

Happold went on to assert that we are now in the midst of a leap epoch in human evolution when consciousness is passing on to a new level of awareness. As a result traditional concepts of God are less and less acceptable. He regarded old images as toppling. A radical new direction therefore has to be taken if we are not to disintegrate in sterile religious culs-de-sac.

About the same time I came across the writings of J.G. Bennett, a scientist and mathematician. In a five-volume work entitled *The Dramatic Universe* (Combe Springs, 1960), Bennett places the 'change' in an even wider context. In a chapter headed 'The Next Age of Mind' he asserts that, 'During the past epoch man has developed and exploited his intellectual powers. A tendency so far scarcely perceptible is towards the awakening of new powers. These will be emotional and intuitive rather than intellectual and analytical.' Here for me was a powerful confirmation of the direction in which I had felt myself moving.

Evolving perceptions of God and humanity

If we are to understand this development and learn how to relate to it we need first to look at some of the historical circumstances which have brought us to our present understanding of humanity and its relationship to Divinity.

Five hundred years before Christ, a Jewish poet and songwriter cried out in an agony of enquiry to his God, 'What are humans that you are mindful of them?' The poet's God was tribal in the fixed limits of His concern, capricious in his unpredictability towards humans and remote in His separateness from human experience. Yet this God who 'inhabited the heavens' held the secret to the meaning of life of earth. Human destiny was in His hands.

Perceptions of this God have evolved and developed with the centuries, and five hundred years onward from the poet's cry the prophets of this hitherto tribal God were proclaiming Him as Lord of all the earth. Yet He was still remote, for His dwelling was in the 'Heavens'. A thousand years later throughout Europe His followers continued to utter the cry for meaning. Life on earth for the vast majority was 'nasty, brutish and cheap', and although their creeds proclaimed a Deity revealed in and through humanity, an understanding of the full significance of this was far into the future. The God towards whom they directed their worship and upon whom they called was still remote and capricious, for prayer addressed to Him might or might not evoke pity. A thousand spires and steeples pointing upward proclaimed to the Western world that their God was above and beyond. His remoteness was largely undiminished.

Not until the eighteenth century AD, were there signs of change in the direction of enquiry concerning the mystery of the human being and indication that faith in the God of the heavens was on the wane. This decline of faith, this turning away, began with the advent of the Industrial Revolution. With the release and harnessing of hitherto undreamed of energies provided by steam and electricity, a new self-awareness, that of dignity and capacity, surfaced in human consciousness, and the realisation of these dimensions of power gave birth to a vision of what it meant to be truly human. The search for answers to the mystery of life began to shift from a Creator God to the creature itself. A remote all-powerful Deity was being forced to surrender its place at the centre of life's stage. For human beings a journey inward had begun. The omnipotence accorded by previous generations to the God above was now perceived to be the prerogative of man, and the proof of His miraculous powers was the new technology. This faith in technology was, as we shall see, eventually to turn in upon itself, but at this stage it indicated a forward movement in the uncovering of knowledge.

Paradoxically this dramatic change of direction was to usher in both a new materialism and eventually a new Self-consciousness. The cry was now heard, 'Glory to man in the highest for man is the master of things.' Yet this was the first step in the Western world towards the uncovering of the multidimensional nature of the human being, a movement which would eventually find its authentic fruition in the coming together of the human and the divine.

The eighteen centuries from the birth of Christ, known in Europe as 'the age of faith', were giving way to that of knowledge. Structures created for the preservation and propagation of belief systems began to crumble. The faithful were losing faith. The time was ripe to look inwards for the unravelling of life's mysteries.

Two significant areas of development emerged at the end of the nineteenth century. The first of these was that of psychological medicine. This was pioneered by Freud and Jung against the weight of established mechanistic views of human nature. Together these two presented to the world a revolutionary view of the human being and of the treatment of disease. The movement which was to establish a psychosomatic basis for many forms of ill health had begun. The effect of human emotions on the subconscious mind – the existence of which was now accepted – and their subsequent effects on physical and mental states were acknowledged to be an area for legitimate investigation. The world of the unconscious had been recognised and was opening up to what was proved to be a scientific method. A universe within had been glimpsed.

The second of these movements developed with a twofold strand, that of Theosophy, the study of the nature of God, and Anthroposophy, the study of the nature of the human. Both had existed from time immemorial in the East but were largely unknown in the West except within the exclusive circles of certain occult societies. The initiator of the Western Theosophical Movement was an extraordinary woman born in the first quarter of the nineteenth century, a Russian, Madame Blavatsky. Her disciple, an equally remarkable woman, Annie Besant, established the Theosophical Society.

Anthroposophy as a system was developed and formulated by Austrian educationalist Rudolf Steiner who related his esoteric studies to every field of human knowledge and endeavour. Such was his genius that on the basis of a vast amount of intuitively acquired knowledge he lectured to doctors on medicine, farmers on agriculture, scientists on science and the clergy on theology.

Steiner's own interpretation of this remarkable capacity was the ability to read what he calls in occult terminology 'the Akashic Records'. (Followers of Carl Jung might see this in terms of tapping in to the Collective Unconscious.) Steiner in *An Outline of Occult Science* (Rudolf Steiner Press, 1964), describes it as follows: 'Anyone who is able to raise his perspective faculty through the visible to the invisible world attains at length a level on which he may see before him what may be compared to a vast spiritual panorama in which are recorded all the past events of the world's history.' Whatever explanation we may give to this, it is clear that Steiner had developed to a very high degree the human capacity for direct or intuitive knowledge.

Both Theosophy and Anthroposophy were from the beginning concerned with the multidimensional nature of humankind and with the world beyond the physical in which we relate through non-physical aspects of our being. According to this understanding a conscious relationship is established with these worlds when the human being's normal sense-bound awareness is changed. Throughout its lifespan the human being, through behaviour patterns, relationships and the direction of its will, is both building up the substance of this non-physical body and the world to which it relates.

Both systems perceive the human being to be a co-creator with God. The traditional understanding of a great gulf fixed between Deity and humanity is bridged. The activity of a God is thus seen to be a continuing and evolving process effected with and through human beings.

The first quarter of the twentieth century confirmed the decline of faith and signalled the great disillusionment with belief in a Divine Providence exercised from afar on behalf of humans. Two World Wars demolished much of the residual hopes in a Divine Omnipotence that ensured the survival of the race. Humans themselves had to ensure a future for the species.

The credibility of God was not always enhanced by His zealous advocates, who frequently overrated His capacity or willingness to intervene in human affairs. As a small boy I went regularly but unwillingly for weekly religious instruction. I recall vividly an occasion when my teacher informed me with deep conviction that whenever I uttered the prayer 'Please God help me' He would immediately do so. I decided to put this to the test. A few days later I arrived home very late from school having been instructed on pain of corporal punishment to come straight home. Confidently I offered the prescribed prayer before marching triumphantly through the front door. Retribution fell swiftly. From that moment onward my teacher's God was dismissed as a failure.

Disillusionment cemented an incipient scepticism. The fallibility of such a God was even more poignantly exposed for me many years later when a colleague who was a devout believer suffered a triple tragedy. The youngest of her children died suddenly of an obscure disease, this, as she said, 'in spite of much prayer'. She bore the loss with courage. Soon afterwards her husband in young middle age died equally suddenly of a heart attack. Again there appeared to be brave acceptance. Then tragedy hit a third time and her son aged twenty-one was killed in a car crash. Then something snapped, the dam burst and torrents of anger poured forth against the 'Interventionist God' in whom she had been taught to believe and who had failed her.

Searching for God in the late twentieth century

The 1960s were to witness fundamental changes in society effected at a speed unparalleled by any other period in the history of Western civilisation. Previously revered institutions and conventions, both religious and secular, were rejected and sometimes demolished in the search for 'honesty and integrity'. 'Freedom' from the shackles of paternalistic structures was sought by the young with a ruthlessness which shocked the older and conservative elements within society. Yet at the heart of this frequently iconoclastic search was a passionate desire to assert the deeply felt conviction that human beings were coming of age and were determined to take control of their own destiny.

Powerful impetus was given to this revolution by a widespread disillusionment with Western science and technology. Achievements previously regarded as signifying the zenith of ingenuity and inventiveness were now acquiring threatening dimensions. What had been regarded as near miraculous technological creations were now seen to contain the seeds of self-destruction. Nuclear power, previously thought to provide the perfect solution to the need for new sources of energy, now appeared to spell out nothing but contamination, both for humans and the planet. In the context of this near revolution a desperate search began for new securities.

Signs of the breadth and intensity of the search were everywhere to be seen, from posters on the London Underground stations projecting images of the latest 'fully realised' gurus from the East, to the offer of crash courses in meditation techniques. Nowhere were there clearer signs of the rising tide of enquiry than in the profusion of new books which were everywhere on sale. The old religious categories in traditional bookshops were giving way to new sections on 'The Occult' and allied subjects. Esoteric literature, for long the life blood of obscure secret societies, became available to the masses.

Astrology returned from the exile it had suffered since the Renaissance and was elevated by many to the status of a serious science. Ancient centres of legend and myth such as Glastonbury, Stonehenge and the island of Iona became the new places of pilgrimage. For those with a penchant for the exotic, ley lines and flying saucers became subjects for endless speculation. Avenues for exploration were endless yet, in spite of many culs-de-sac of curiosity and superstition, at the heart of it all was a serious search.

The spearhead of this search was to be found in the 'New Age' centres which began first of all to appear in the United Kingdom. At this early stage, largely a phenomenon of the English-speaking world, they spread rapidly to the USA, Australia and New Zealand. Later they were to come to birth in most countries of Europe.

The centres had no common organisation, but were held together by a shared aim and vision. They differed widely in form and structure, and operated both in town and country. Usually a resident core group held the community together. Visitors were received to share in the common life and take part in workshops and educational programmes. These communities ranged in scope and size from the widely known Findhorn Community in Scotland to numerous tiny groups, hidden away in obscure corners and known only to the network of seekers whom they attracted.

Each centre had its own particular emphasis. Their undertakings embraced all aspects of education. One thing held in common was the desire to encourage genuine seekers to believe in the possibility of change, both in individuals and in society, and to effect the awakening of those faculties generally ignored by conventional systems of education, namely the imagination and intuition. The teachings of the great mystics, often referred to as the 'Masters of Wisdom', figured prominently in their training programmes.

How may the significance of these centres be assessed? At best they developed virtues long thought of as inextricably tied to religious belief systems and proved that their 'Techniques of Transformation' worked, that is they effected positive change in the human character. In a non-religious setting they touched the very heart of religion. By the 1980s many of these centres had disappeared, yet in their day they were significant catalysts for a positive shift in human consciousness and cultivated impulses which belong to our time.

In the late 1970s I received an invitation to visit a thriving centre in the Cotswolds. Based in a lovely old farmhouse, its particular concern was to promote the study of the vision of the great mystic Muhyiddin Ibn Arabi, who was born in Spain in 1165.

Ibn Arabi was both a renowned scholar and theologian, but was pre-eminently an exponent of experiential wisdom. The focus of the study group which I attended was Arabi's assertion that 'He who knows himself knows also his Lord'. Yet this study was far from being an arid intellectual pursuit and there was an assumption behind the teaching technique that all taking part were both teachers and learners. All were given the opportunity to speak and to share their immediate perceptions. There was no discussion, but whilst one spoke all the others gave him or her their full attention.

This was a very powerful experience for me; it was the sharing at a very deep level which enabled me to touch the group.

The Eastern contribution

During this period wise men came from the East, gurus of many kinds. They spoke a language of spirituality which differed sharply from that of Western religious thought. Foremost among them was the Maharishi who enlisted his disciples, prominent among them the Beatles, into schools of transcendental meditation. The search for a God was taking the form of a quest for 'Self-realisation'.

For those seekers who resonated with this search for the 'higher Self' and whose commitment to the journey was serious and dedicated, the Russian George Ivanovitch Gurdjieff became a clear signpost. Gurdjieff, born in the Caucasas in 1880, spent all his adult life until his death in 1949 in a restless search to discover the secret of human transformation.

The human being was, Gurdjieff insisted, a machine. All its actions, thoughts and so-called convictions are the result of external stimuli. Basic to his training methods were intensive study, self-observation, physical work and sacred dance. All this was directed to the awakening of true potential. Humans, he insisted, differ from animals only in one respect – given the will they are able to find true 'selfhood'. When consciousness begins to centre in the true self, as distinct from our many personality selves, the work of transformation begins. We awaken from a sleep of death. Unknown beyond a small circle of disciples during his lifetime, since his death his teachings are increasingly disseminated and followed in the Western world.

New images of God

Parallel to this widespread evolution of consciousness were movements within and peculiar to the religious institutions themselves, movements concerned with new images of God.

In the late 1950s loud whispers were heard, uttered by a popular writer and Biblical scholar, thought at that time to be very radical, J.B. Phillips. He declared that the God of the Churches was becoming too small to have any credibility in a world that was beginning to glimpse vistas of outer space. In his book *Your God Is Too Small* (Wyvern Press, 1956) Phillips writes in the Introduction:

> *It often appears to those outside the churches that if Christians are not strenuously defending an outgrown conception of God they are cherishing a hothouse God who could only exist between the pages of the Bible or inside the four walls of a church.*

The seeds of new thought had been effectively sown and ten years later both the religious and secular world were precipitated into widespread debate by the book *Honest to God* (SCM Press, 1965) written by a Bishop of the Church, John Robinson. The bishop's thesis (based on the ideas of Paul Tillich in *The Courage To Be*, Yale University Press, 1977) was to set forth God not as above and apart from humanity but 'as the very ground of man's being'. This evoked tremendous public response in the UK, both in reactions from sections of the 'faithful' who saw this as a direct attack against cherished truth, and from those who could no longer with integrity continue with the old image of an out-of-date God.

At the same time hundreds of letters to the press confirmed the feelings of liberation which many readers had experienced. Perhaps the book's greatest significance is to be seen not in the asserting of something new and novel, but rather that for a great many people it brought into consciousness something that had been known intuitively for a very long time. It perfectly articulated what they were experiencing and took the lid off the religious situation, bringing great release from the bondage of the past.

Sadly the tide of establishment reaction quickly flowed over the new path that was being opened up. Few were ready and able to give clear leadership and the bishop and his book faded from public consciousness.

Just prior to this I had been appointed Chaplain to the British Embassy Church in Vienna, the romantic city which at that time had become a favourite stopping-off place for young people travelling East in search of 'enlightenment'. Many of these would meet on Sunday evening in the crypt of the church for discussion. The bishop's book became an obvious subject for debate. One young man *en route* to India concluded one such session with the words: 'If God is really the ground of my being then I need travel no further.'

Inevitably the definition of God in this apparently novel way was the starting point for the following week's debate. To say that God is the ground of my being is all very well, said the group leader, but doesn't that leave Him as rather faceless? 'Not at all,' responded a young Jewish student, obviously familiar with his Scriptures. That problem was sorted out long ago when God appeared to Moses the Leader of the Jewish people.' For Moses, confronted with the apparent impersonality and facelessness of a God who manifested as flames in a burning bush, asked the pertinent question 'Who are you?' To which came the reply 'I AM that I AM' which, loosely interpreted, meant, 'I am known by what I am proved to be!' Experiential wisdom indeed.

Feminism and holism

With the rise of the feminist movement came the question of God's gender. When Christabel Pankhurst advised her suffragettes to 'trust in God and She will help you' hers was a lone voice crying in the wilderness. The God of the monotheistic religions – Judaism, Christianity and Islam – was unquestionably male. Yet an inevitable result of the feminist movement in the West has been a powerful and increasingly effective assault upon what may be regarded as the last bastion of male domination and chauvinism, the Deity itself. Since the early 1980s groups of the faithful have dared to incorporate into their forms of worship the concept of a Mother God. Again there has been a powerful reaction. Nevertheless the movement continues to gather momentum. The God of 'the heavens and the earth' has revealed a dual gender.

Significant within the context of our examination of an evolving God is that of the holistic movement which came into prominence in Europe and the United States in the 1970s and 1980s. At last medicine and science were beginning to view the human being not as a mechanical construction in which the causes of breakdown or malfunction should be sought for in all the separate parts. Both mind and emotions began to be seen as essentially related and parts of a whole.

Yet the holistic concept is less than true to itself if it fails to take into recognition that aspect of the human being which alone can bring body, intellect and emotions into an integrated whole. It is as we cultivate this potential step by step that we shall begin to touch at a very deep level the mystery which constitutes the human being. Then we shall know experientially that which the mystics of all religions and none have always known, namely that the realisation of our full humanity is to touch divinity. This is the true journey inward, the journey we are about to take.

The journey is a meditative one. Meditation and its centrality in the unfolding of the path will become clear as we move forward. We begin with the cultivation of body consciousness.

MEDITATION ON YOUR BODY

The start of the journey places you immediately within the centre of paradox, for to travel in this manner − i.e., to pursue the journey inwards − requires at the same time that you mentally and physically stand still. This standing still is, as it were, to be poised at the starting point and is an acknowledgement of your own personhood as focused and realised in your body.

The importance of this giving of space, time and recognition to your physical form cannot be over-emphasised. Most of us at some time or other have wished that our bodies were other than they are. Nevertheless, as they are they represent a pattern of God-given energies expressed in unique form. All the intangible and tangible elements which constitute your total being are represented there. It is through the body that they can reveal themselves. Your body makes explicit all that is implicit within. In recognising this you are affirming your true identity.

Do not try to analyse or intellectualise this. Many of us are heavily conditioned by culture or education to underestimate or ignore the physical body's potential as a window into our total being. It is important that we now begin to open this window experientially.

Without selectivity or judgement I affirm through my physical being my very self, and in doing so find a measure of detachment from those superimposed identities which the conditioning of birth, education and the pressures of life have imposed upon me. It is also a letting go of those false images which I have so often projected to achieve real or imagined acceptance with others.

My body is the outward and visible form of all those realities which together make up my identity. It holds a legacy from the past, potential for the future and above all it declares the possibility of the present moment. It cannot be overvalued.

Some aspects of my body's significance I can know consciously, others are hidden deep within and below the level of consciousness. The concern at this stage is not to know or to judge them but rather to see the body as an immediate and recognisable sign of hidden treasures.

All religions pay homage to the body and in a variety of ways recognise it as expressing in time and space aspects of the Divine image. According to the Christian tradition the body is a 'Temple of the Holy Spirit'. Hindus recognise it as a vehicle of the Higher Self. For the Buddhist it is the point from which reality is discerned. In Islam the body reflects the Glory of Allah, and the Jewish Scriptures tell us that God created man in His own image.

It is then within and through my body that I find the meeting-point between the human and the Divine. William Blake, the eighteenth-century English mystic, using the imagery of Judaism, expressed this as follows:

> *I give you the end of a golden string*
> *Only wind it into a ball*
> *It will lead you in at Heaven's gate*
> *Close by Jerusalem's wall.*

> Jerusalem – the Emanation
> of the Giant Albion

POSITIONING YOUR BODY

You pass now from thinking about the body to the practice of a simple exercise which will enable you to feel and express body-consciousness.

Take up a sitting position which allows you to be relaxed yet alert. For most of us the natural position is sitting in a chair with an upright back. Lying down would most likely produce somnolence! Having taken up a comfortable position, become aware of different parts of your body and consciously place them where and how you want them to be. Feet should either be placed soles flat against the floor or tucked beneath the chair. Allow the hands to rest unclenched in your lap. The eyes should be closed.

There should be no hurriedness about this exercise. Take it slowly step by step, aware of what you are doing.

Holding the head as erect as possible will help you feel expectant. Now in your mind's eye see your body and reverence it. You may find it helpful to repeat to yourself a sentence such as: 'I have a beautiful God-given body and I reverence it.'

Keep the picture of your body in your mind's eye and be conscious that your body is talking to you. It has a language of its own, clearly understandable if we are prepared to listen. The clenched hands, the tense thighs and the taut brow are all saying 'release me that I might serve you properly'.

RELAXING YOUR BODY

Beginning with the crown of your head, consciously relax the muscles of the crown and face. You may find it helpful to relate this to your breathing. So as you breathe out let the tensions ride away on the outbreath. Do the same with shoulders, waist – giving particular attention to the solar plexus area – thighs, legs and feet. Having completed this at a leisurely pace then breathe as it were through all the pores of your body, letting go of all tensions. If any particular area tightens up again, gently repeat the relaxing technique.

Look again with your mind's eye at the whole of your body. Again reverence it. Focus your attention on the centre of the chest, representing the deep centre of your being, and slowly repeat the words:

I am a child of the Universe. I have a right to be.

How long should the exercise last? I suggest at this stage that you practise for ten minutes in the morning and the same again in the evening.

Twenty minutes each day will without any doubt bring not only a new body awareness, but the quiet mind which will begin to form within will reflect something of the God who 'is known by what He proves Himself to be'.

> *There is an inmost centre in us all*
> *Where truth abides in fullness: and around*
> *Wall upon wall, the gross flesh hems it in,*
> *That perfect clear perception – which is truth.*
> *A baffling and perverting carnal mesh*
> *Binds it, and makes all error: and to KNOW*
> *Rather consists in opening out a way*
> *Whence the imprisoned splendour may escape,*
> *Than in effecting entry for a light*
> *Supposed to be without.*
>
> ROBERT BROWNING, 'Paracelsus'

3

The Fully Human Being

A man has many skins in himself, covering the depths of his
   heart.
Man knows so many things; he does not know himself.
Go into your own ground and learn to know yourself there.

MEISTER ECKHART

During the rush-hour on a busy London railway station an
obviously bewildered and lost-looking traveller button-holed a
commuter struggling through the evening throng and pleaded
for help in proceeding to a well known Midlands town. After a
brief reflection back came the reply, 'Really I am not sure, but
I'm fairly certain you don't start from here!'

Such is frequently the dilemma today of those desiring to
find a spiritual path, and such the ambiguity of response to
enquiry. As the twenty-first century breaks upon the Western
world a profusion of new cults, the undiminished claims of
competing gurus and the oft-repeated anathema of religious
authorities leave the would-be pilgrim not only confused but
almost convinced that some demanding steps, some tremendous
leap of faith must be taken before the promise of salvation or
enlightenment can be achieved.

The place where we are at, the condition in which
the present finds us, is not apparently recognised as a proper
starting-point. In all probability a prerequisite for beginning

the journey is that of incorporation into a group or at the very least attachment to a teacher. Added to this is the frequent necessity of learning a new language, religious, mystical or psychological.

The sum total of such demands often adds up to a social dislocation, an alienation from our cultural roots and a denigration of at least part of our very identity. The acceptable beginning of such a journey requires a dramatic shift, not only in thinking but quite often geographically. 'Holy' places and 'holy' people are declared to be *de rigueur* objects of pilgrimage. All this re-enforces the thinking that where I am now as a mentally, emotionally and physically operating human being is not the appropriate place of beginning for a valid and fulfilling spiritual journey. Nothing could be further from the truth. For our journey begins not with submission to a package deal of 'truth', but rather in the awakening of faculties of perception.

The great thirst for such awakening which characterised the 1960s and the 1970s caused many young seekers to travel eastwards and particularly to India. It was as if a strong migratory impulse was propelling them towards what many interpreted as their authentic roots. A powerful homing instinct was exercising a compulsion to find their true selves.

In their desire for what became known, for the first time in the West, as Self-realisation a sometimes frenetic search for a 'perfect master' was being pursued. Without doubt this pilgrimage from the West to the East was prompted by the apparent inability of the churches in Europe either to hear the questions that were being asked or, when hearing them, to understand. 'Spirituality', which is what the search and the questioning was all about, was generally speaking regarded as a poor relation of the study of religion. So with some striking exceptions the churches closed their doors and turned their backs.

The full story of the great migration has yet to be told. Sadly there was often an unrealistic picture. India is a land of many parts. Its spirituality co-exists with material poverty. Because of the spiritual poverty of the West the East appeared from afar off to be metaphorically the 'land of milk and honey'. Fired with enthusiasm fed by the visits of gurus, many added to their search a new asceticism. They travelled overland, often enduring appalling hardships. Some disappeared, never to be heard of again. Others encountered only disillusionment and deception. The most intrepid trekked as far as the Himalayas, the home of the great *rishis* or god-men, for they, it was believed, had the ability to transmit spiritual energy to others, a power that would initiate into the way of enlightenment.

Yet in spite of widespread illusion and disillusionment there were those who found fulfilment and spiritual awakening. Holy men and women were encountered and the reality of a universal spirituality transcending doctrine and dogma was experienced.

I talked in the late 1980s to one such fulfilled seeker, then in middle life. To 'follow the call' as he had understood it he had left his family and abandoned his studies. After travelling for nine months he arrived eventually at a Hindu ashram in south India. In 'that holy place,' he said, 'I stayed for only one week. No longer was necessary. For the master there said only one thing. He quoted the words of Jesus: "Let those who have ears hear" and "The kingdom of Heaven is within you". I returned immediately to the West with new eyes and new ears. I recognise now in my own country signs of a universal spirituality.'

About that time I recall walking in the grounds of an ancient monastery with the Abbess, a woman with an aged body which contained the heart of a child. I asked her to tell me about her early years as a nun. 'Then I must go back at least fifty years,' she said with a smile. She told me how half a century before, as a young novice on a warm summer's day, she lay on her back in the convent orchard looking at the apple blossom and feeling sad as she pondered on the fact that 'all beauty is transient and must eventually die'. 'Then suddenly,' she said, 'I heard a voice saying "look". "But I am looking," I replied. Then the voice said, "But look with the eyes of your heart". At that moment,' said the Abbess, 'I saw the reality, the unfading beauty and unity behind all created things. A new faculty had awakened within me, something beyond my understanding, yet it was pure joy.' She was silent for a while, then sighed and said, 'But as my religious training proceeded the faculty died within me.'

So as we take the first step on our journey we look at the question 'Why is such an awakening necessary and what is its nature?'

New dimensions

From the moment of birth we are conditioned to operate in a three-dimensional world. These are functionally its clearly defined limits – limits imposed by space, time and educational programmes. From birth to death the normal lifespan is contained within and conditioned by these barriers. Within this context human consciousness is nurtured. It is contained in space and regulated by time. These limits are reinforced by educational systems which generally speaking recognise these boundaries as absolute. We are thus encapsulated within the world of the five senses. These are seen as the only guide to reality. A prison-house is created within which the vast majority of human beings with varying degrees of satisfaction are content to live out their lives.

Yet the story of humanity clearly indicates a long history of humans continually probing to extend themselves beyond the limits of this prison-house and to cultivate an understanding of themselves which takes into consideration dimensions beyond the world of the senses. It is this unceasing search which has given rise both to philosophy and religion. Philosophy may be described as rational reflection on experience, and religion as belief in the human as a spiritual being. Yet, significant as both have been in the evolution of human consciousness, neither the reflections of philosophy nor religious beliefs can of themselves take us experientially beyond encapsulation within three-dimensional existence.

In spite of this, history is resplendent with men and women

who, with great diversity of motivations, have fought valiantly to occupy a 'larger space', i.e., to extend their experience of life and to awaken to new dimensions of living.

It is into this larger space that your present journey is leading you. And this depends not on any special ability nor unusual gifts, nor indeed does it require superhuman aptitude. It is a readiness to release your potential. For contained within your ordinary humanity is all that constitutes what is uniquely you, a humanity to be fulfilled.

Few people in the Western world have not heard of Helen Keller. Born blind and deaf, this remarkable woman nevertheless achieved fame by the development of alternative faculties of perception. In the course of her life she acquired a high degree of academic excellence and the capacity to communicate effectively to vast audiences. Such an attainment powerfully demonstrates the fact that human potential and capacity for understanding cannot be limited to hearing with the ears and seeing with the eyes. There is for all of us, and for all of us now just as we are, the possibility of awakening the most powerful of all human facilities, the capacity to look 'with the eyes of the heart'. Yet such looking, such awakening must be seen within the context of the whole human potential. So the second question we must also examine is our total capacity to acquire knowledge.

Three areas of knowledge

All of us have access to three areas of knowledge. The first is that which is called instinctive. It is accumulated knowledge, inherent in varying degrees within all human beings. It has been acquired through aeons of evolution, imprinted upon the racial memory and stored in the subconscious mind. Such knowledge comes into consciousness through external emotional stimuli. Its operation is involuntary. This knowledge is also shared with the animal kingdom which defends itself, preserves life and reacts to aggression without premeditated thought. Such responses and reactions have no moral content. They are automatic and conditioned. Fear and self-preservation figure predominantly in this area of knowledge.

The second area of knowledge is that which we call rational. It consists of information received through the senses from the 'natural world'. Its evaluation is by the process of logical deduction and it is called 'reasonable'. It provides the basis for scientific, philosophical and frequently religious understanding of the nature of truth. As we have seen, it provides the framework for all recognised educational systems.

The third area of knowledge is intuitive. It is this capacity with which we are concerned. As with instinct, the operation of this faculty is frequently involuntary. Yet it is fundamentally different from the instinctive, with which it is often confused, for it is never a conditioned response. Its development runs parallel to true spiritual awakening. It is therefore conditional on the right focusing of the will and operates from a place of inner freedom. It is a faculty of direct cognition. It is not based upon previous experience, nor is it attained through the process of reasoning. Knowledge or understanding acquired in this manner can be received in no other way and is concerned with ultimate reality. From this it will be seen that this third capacity and potential, the capacity for direct knowledge, is the faculty which we need to awaken in order to begin our journey.

Opening the doors of perception

Is there for each of us a time to awaken, and are there 'days of opportunity' given to us for opening the doors of perception? I have no doubt that this is so and that such opportunity comes to us in an infinite variety of ways. The 'chance' encounter, familiar words heard in a new way – the means by which the need is recognised are beyond counting.

In my own life such a time came to me during a visit to the holy island of Iona off the coast of Scotland. The occasion was the concluding gathering of a week's conference. The final prayers had been offered and the blessing proclaimed. In the aisle of a packed Abbey I turned to my companion and complained of inaudibility, lack of articulation and of any dramatic ability to communicate on the part of the last participant. The reply was gentle but immediate and devastating in its effects. The words echoed those of Jesus Christ addressed to the scholars who could not understand him, 'You have eyes and you do not see, you have ears and you do not hear. Are you not aware of what is happening in this place?' In that moment of truth and confrontation I knew that I was not. And I knew why. For my expectations and perceptions were limited to and enclosed within the five senses. This was no instant enlightenment. I knew only that I did not know and that the time for a new process of learning had come.

It was to facilitate and make provision for training in this learning process that the community to which I belong, the 'Omega Order', was founded in 1980. The Vision which has inspired the Order is that of an evolving universe at the heart of which are committed human beings, struggling to fulfil their role as the conscious spearhead of this evolutionary process. This struggle is the bringing to birth of their full humanity. The philosophy embodying this understanding is expressed in the *Omega Vision*.

I quote from what I have written elsewhere of the finding of this door:

> *Those who would know that world and enter in*
> *Must first the entrance find*
> *And here the paradox is great;*
> *For finding this and moving out beyond*
> *The limitations which have till now*
> *Constricted and constrained us*
> *We find a coming home.*

And all this must we find ourselves, within ourselves,
And for that finding know – the readiness is all
But how create a readiness to circumvent
The senses, take the barrier down
And draw aside the veils?

The answer lies within the space already there –
Ourselves within, but do not think that space
To be the world of thought or deep untried emotion
These two do both indeed exist, and in the first there lurks
The ever ready power of self delusion
Where thoughts feed thoughts – divorced from all but thinking.

And in the second fantasies do readily spring up
To take the guise of deep and fervent faith.
The one who longs to see the vision –
And if we do not 'long' we're not yet ready
Must now begin to find beyond these two
The place of clear perception:
The space to see, to be, to move and quickly to outgrow

Those limitations which the pattern of our living
Has imposed upon us.

The End of an Age (Darton, Longman
and Todd, 1983)

It was said of an Indian Master of the spiritual life that he
would accept no one as a disciple who was still wrestling
with emotional problems, as this blocked the way to opening
the door of perception. The imposition of such a condition
would, we might feel, effectively exclude most of us from
embarking on the path of spiritual awakening. The recognition of the emotional dimension of our being is important
and attempts to ignore or repress this can only result in frustration. Yet battling with the emotions can very often
become counter-productive. We come out of the battlefield

at the very point where we entered in. An old nineteenth-century hymn contains the line 'If you tarry till you are better you will never come at all'. Therapy groups, co-counselling, dynamic encounters and methods of producing emotional catharsis can all become effective release mechanisms, but none of this should be confused with the opening of that door deep within ourselves which leads to perceiving the way forward. Resolution of emotional problems is important, yet equally so is the learning to stand back from them and to know that if the journey upon which we are embarking is through the door of the heart, then emotional problems which may arise will come into controllable focus, as it were in parenthesis to our chosen spiritual path.

The heart centre

Let us look a little closer at the space 'beyond' those occupied and represented by emotions and thoughts. Frequently called the 'heart' centre, it is not of course to be identified with the physical heart. Yet the human heart, which is the focal point of life for the physical body, well represents it. I have already referred to it as the free space, 'the place of clear perception'. In esoteric terminology it is sometimes described as the Heart Chakra, from the Sanskrit 'wheel' or vortex of energy. It is well described as a 'free' space, as distinct from the solar plexus which represents the reactionary instinctive space. All descriptions of those dimensions of the human being beyond physical manifestation must be tentative, and are useful only as far as they provide a working framework to encourage development toward an integration of the human being as a whole, a human being fulfilled within itself, in relation to others and to the planet.

In Chapter 1 we made the assertion that to realise our full humanity is to touch divinity. And here we find ourselves within a paradox. For on one hand the word divinity or God postulates an otherness than the human being, and on the other is the undoubted fact that it is only from the centre of human experience that the door to perception of 'godliness' can be opened.

As a young enthusiastic and optimistic teacher of divinity I recall setting an examination paper for a class of young people preparing for religious initiation. They were all in their early teens. The examination followed a series of instruction classes in which there had been a study of the Mosaic Law, i.e., the Ten Commandments. 'What,' I posed as question number one, 'is the first and great commandment?' My anticipation of what I had foolishly thought to be the obviously correct answer was rudely shattered when on opening the first paper I read: 'I must have none other Gods but ME!' Blasphemous? Ludicrous? Or a pointer to a profound truth? Clearly in that context and for religious students of that age there could be only one response on the part of the teacher, i.e., 'You have got it quite wrong.' In the context of today's awakening to the God factor 'within', it is my conviction that we can risk what may be regarded as an idolatrous caricature, and see this looking into ourselves, this awareness of our true identity, as recognition as to where lie the very seeds of our divinity.

Are there then clear and definite steps which we can take to focus consciousness on that dimension of our being?

Many generations of children have been entranced by the story of the Sleeping Princess. Like all parables it is both for children and the childlike. At the heart of a fortress lies the highly desirable and beautiful Princess, surrounded by the all but impenetrable thickets. Only a Prince's sword can cut a way through. There at the very centre the Princess is awakened by a kiss. Its message is both simple and profound. Those who will penetrate the innermost centre where true union is to be effected must first penetrate the barriers erected by the incessantly chattering intellect and the pressurising emotions.

At the conclusion of this chapter is a meditational exercise which takes us step by step through the barriers to that place where as we have seen 'truth abides in fullness'.

Awareness

It is helpful at this stage to realise that a two-way process has been initiated with the very recognition of this faculty of perception. By the giving of time and space to the recognition of this capacity we are informing our subconscious and in return it reassures us. The overall effect of this is a powerful contribution to the cultivation of awareness.

What is it exactly that we become aware of? Let us look again at the experience of the Abbess in the orchard. The revelation which came to this young nun was not primarily to do with the fact of a permanent unfading beauty represented in the physical world by apple blossom, but rather what she perceived as the essential unity behind all created things. It is this awareness of being an essential part of the whole, a whole that spells out meaning and purpose for each individual, which breaks into consciousness as 'direct knowledge'. And let us be clear that this is no abstract information to titillate the imagination, nor is it knowledge to be stored up in the intellect as if to add another book to an already well stocked library. The knowledge of which we become aware is that which speaks to our immediate condition and real need.

At this point in your journey it can be helpful to the process of realising your identity to think and feel the personal pronoun 'I'. For here, in my own space, I am making my own conscious movement forward.

By a conscious decision and a decisive commitment I move into a new space. From the confines of the senses through an exercise of my will I open a door leading to a larger world than I have hitherto known, and find this to be both a reaching out and a coming home, a stepping into the unknown and an entering in to a new security. I am coming home.

Whilst travelling in New Zealand I was invited to visit a Maori Meeting House, a kind of Community Centre. Several religions were represented. I understood very little of what was going on around me. From the language to the food, all was new and strange. Yet from the moment of entering the building I had the feeling that I had come home. I shared this with a friend and asked why this should be so. 'Because,' he replied, 'this is a heart-centred place.'

To move into this space is to extend myself beyond those self-erected barriers which have until now restricted my experience of life. It is a return to the very Source of my being, and to know that I am a child of the Universe at the heart of which is a loving concern for me and for all humanity. I know that the 'unity of all things' is a unity which encompasses my whole being. As my journey opens up before me the implications of entering into and operating from this space will unfold stage by stage.

We referred earlier to some of the demands made upon searchers for a spiritual path. What are the demands of this journey inwards? All that is necessary is the self-imposed discipline of a commitment to move forward on the 'straight path'.

All movement forward implies also a leaving behind. This we shall act out in imagination in the meditative exercise at the end of this chapter.

During my youth I spent five years in India. My initial task upon arrival was to set about learning Hindi and for the first year I spent eight hours a day grappling with the language. At that time it was very much the fashion to follow the 'direct method', i.e., not to concentrate on learning grammatical constructions, but to learn as a child learns language – to speak it. So I was, as it were, thrown in at the deep end and made to learn by practice.

In order to see and to learn from the heart it is necessary to practise the disciplines of looking and listening, and to learn by practice.

Signposts for understanding

We now need to pause and consider the ground we have covered. First of all we remind ourselves that the acquiring of information is not to be identified with progress along the path. It may be helpful to see the information offered in the first part of each chapter as an oasis or resting-place where we find signposts, lines of thought which may lead us beyond themselves to further progress.

During a visit to India I visited a well known ashram, a place where East and West, Christianity and Hinduism meet in the unity of common experience. I entered the meditation room and, after sitting and absorbing the atmosphere for some time, I noticed a sign which read 'You are asked not to read in this room'. I was both pleased and surprised. My Western orientation did not easily come to terms with the fact that what is sometimes called 'Holy reading' quickly mitigates against touching the reality described by study. Such reading quickly becomes counter-productive and leads to the self-deception which confuses 'I know' with 'I know about'. To learn about discernment is not to discern. To acknowledge that inherent within my humanity are unused and undeveloped faculties is not to develop or to use them.

We need, then, at this stage, to use our God-given capacities to understand ourselves and also to learn how to exercise these gifts.

At a later stage in our journey we shall consider how these faculties operate in relation to various meditative practices. Just now, standing as I am on the threshold of an 'entering in' experience, I need simply to be aware of my common inheritance as a fully human being.

MEDITATION EXERCISE

In this second exercise in meditation read slowly the sections headed 'Reflection', 'Imagination' and 'Intuition'. Then repeat the relaxation process ('Relaxing my body') explained at the end of Chapter 2.

In this exercise we move from body-consciousness to heart-centredness. In order to become easily familiar with the relaxation process which is the basis of every exercise, you will find it helpful to go through this from time to time as an extra exercise in itself. And remember that these are not practice runs. Every exercise, every period of time, however short, set apart for learning to be still is part of the growing process. They are steps along the way.

REFLECTION

I begin, then, by reflecting and considering the fact that in the exercise of my full humanity I have both the privilege and the right to enter into that space described in the *Omega Vision* as 'the space to see, to be, to move quickly to outgrow those limitations which the pattern of our living has imposed upon us'.

This reflective understanding of my potential and opportunity is capable of a 'proving process', i.e., that of inner resonance with this assertion. We shall come experientially to this process as we proceed step by step in this exercise.

IMAGINATION

To imagine creatively is not, as is sometimes thought, to escape into a kind of self-indulgent day-dreaming. Rather is it to see reality in symbolic form. So I now see myself as a pilgrim standing at the entrance to a world of possibilities, perceptions and privileges. The door is wide open and I am bidden to enter. All this I see imaginatively in my mind's eye.

But, aware as I am of welcome and an immediacy of opportunity, I am also conscious of being weighed down by heavy baggage. This baggage consists of a vast assortment of ghosts from the past: half-buried memories; wounds inflicted on my self and upon others; unfulfilled dreams; opportunities missed; relationships unresolved; and the present loneliness born of clinging to the past.

Now is not the time to dig further into the baggage, nor should you succumb to the temptation to reflect upon the contents. We face two questions, both of which we pose ourselves. 'Can I embrace the freedom which leaving my baggage behind will give me? Can I put it down now?'

During a conducted retreat I once led a group on an imaginative journey progressing through great varieties of scenery to the top of a high mountain. The journey began with a leaving behind of all that might impede progress. Following the exercise the participants were invited to share their experience of this imaginative exercise. One woman responded, 'I was quite happy to travel but I wanted to be quite sure of getting back to my encumbrances, so I tied handkerchiefs on trees and bushes all along the way, to guide me back!'

It may well be that we want to retrace our steps. There may be a returning and another letting go. What we can be quite sure of is that a letting go now will make future letting go much easier.

INTUITION

The third gift of my humanity is to know intuitively. The exercise of this faculty may cause me to acknowledge paradoxically: 'I know what I know. How I know it I do not know and I know not how to express it.'

It is towards and with this knowledge that we now move in

our meditational exercise, and in this we build upon the 'body-consciousness' into which we entered at the conclusion of Chapter 2. So, as before, step by step in a systematic yet relaxed manner I go through the process of relaxing my body, beginning with the head and stage by conscious stage proceeding to the breathing away of tensions through all the pores of the body.

CENTRING IN THE HEART

I again centre my consciousness in the chest. Then I become conscious that the space represented by my heart, the deep centre of my being, is a place of light. For a few minutes I let myself be conscious of the light as it spreads from the heart throughout my whole body.

I become in understanding, in imagination and with deep knowing a creature of the Light.

God said, 'Let there be Light, and there was Light.'

4

The Awakened Heart

We can only love that we know, and we can never know completely what we do not love. Love is a mode of knowledge, and when the love is sufficiently disinterested and sufficiently intense, the knowledge becomes unitive knowledge and so takes on the quality of infallibility. Where there is no disinterested love there is only biased self love, and consequently only a partial and distorted knowledge, both of the self, and of the world of things, lives, minds and spirit outside of the self.

ALDOUS HUXLEY, *The Perennial Philosophy*
(Chatto & Windus, 1980)

The first steps on our journey have brought us to the point of focusing upon that space within our consciousness which we call the heart. This is not to be identified with the physical heart, but this organ of our body well represents the core or centre of our being.

The confirmation that you are learning to centre in this space is the development of inner knowing, a bringing into consciousness of that which in your subconscious you have always known. You are beginning to know that there is very much more to your being and your personhood than 'science and the senses' have decided. You are waking up to 'mystical consciousness'. What is this consciousness, and how may it develop?

'He who seeks to follow the way of the opened heart is indeed a mystic.' So states W.T. Stace in his book *The Teachings of the Mystics* (New American Library, 1960). But what exactly is a mystic and how does one define mysticism? Many thousands of books have sought to describe the essential nature of the authentic mystical experience. Such descriptions are inevitably coloured by the cultural, religious and psychological predispositions and training of the writer.

Evelyn Underhill, an English mystic and prolific writer on the subject in the early part of this century, poses this question and, aware that she might be accused of over-simplification, gives the following definition: 'Mysticism is the art of union with reality. The mystic is a person who has attained that union in a greater or lesser degree; or who aims at and believes in such attainment' (*Practical Mysticism for Normal People*, Dent, 1914). Such a definition cuts across all the accretions of theological speculation and effectively denudes the subject of a spurious and romantic mystery. Again risking the charge of over-simplification, I would go a step further and reduce the description to the two words used by F.C. Happold, i.e., 'experiential wisdom'.

What mysticism is not

However, because of the widespread confusion in the West today concerning the nature of mysticism, it is perhaps necessary to clear away some common misconceptions and to say what mysticism is not.

Let us begin by making clear that it has nothing whatever to do with the occult. The mystic and the occultist, i.e., those who explore the hidden world of what is commonly called magic, are quite different people. It has nothing to do with parapsychological phenomena, such as telepathy, telekinesis, clairvoyance or precognition. These and allied subjects are not mystical phenomena. In following the mystical path it is not uncommon that these particular powers manifest, but they are not part of and must be clearly distinguished from authentic mysticism. Conversely, those who have travelled far along the path of the mystic may experience none of these powers. Visions have nothing to do with, though they may happen to, the mystic.

In the second half of this century there have been a number of alleged visions of the Virgin Mary in many different parts of the world. Such claims may or may not be authentic. They cannot be described as 'mystical'. This is also true of the visions of a number of well known historical characters. Joan of Arc is such a person. She may or may not have been a mystic, but this has nothing to do with her hearing of voices.

Teresa of Avila, the great Spanish mystic in the sixteenth century, experienced visions but made it quite clear that this was not what she was seeking as she developed her inner life. Indeed she said of some of these visions that they may have been 'sent by Satan' to deceive her. She was also seen to levitate at her altar, to which extraordinary experience she responded with some impatience, 'Put me down, Lord!'

Teresa's contemporary, St John of the Cross, specifically warned his followers not to seek for visions nor to be misled by them if they occured. They were not, he emphasised, to be confused with true mystical union.

In modern times the well known spiritual leader in India, Sai Baba, has many times demonstrated to his followers and sceptics alike his possession of supernormal powers, and undoubtedly he is regarded by many as a mystic. This may be so, but he himself has made it clear on many occasions that the performance of miracles has no essential place in the spiritual journey.

What mysticism is

I have proposed as a definition of the mystical path 'experiential wisdom', yet this requires some qualification, for the very word 'experience' may become misleading. It is of the very essence of the mystical consciousness that is non-sensuous. It cannot therefore be described as an emotional 'experience', for it is formless, shapeless, colourless, odourless and soundless. For this reason the word 'experience' must be used with caution. A vision has to do with visual imagery having shape and colour. A voice is an auditory image. Both visions and voices are therefore sensuous experiences.

How then may we describe this mystical consciousness which is void of all sensations and contains neither concepts nor emotions? So far we have looked at what this consciousness is not. Can we say what it is? What can be said is that what we are endeavouring to describe is to do with the spiritual world, beyond time and space – that dimension which we touch and enter into through the awakening of the heart.

Is it possible to conceive of a consciousness that is devoid of all intellectual and emotional content? In his book *The Varieties of Religious Experience* (Penguin, new edn. 1983) William James suggests as a result of his psychological researches that

> our normal consciousness, rational consciousness, as we call it is but one special type of consciousness, whilst all about it, parted from it by the flimsiest of screens there lie potential forms of consciousness entirely different.

W.T. Stace comments upon this as follows in *Teachings of the Mystics*:

> We may think of this as being like a building with three floors. The ground floor consists of physical sensations – sights, sounds, smells, taste, touch sensations. The second floor consists of images which we tend to think of as mental copies of sensations. The third floor is the level of the intellect which is the faculty of concepts. On this floor we find abstract thinking and reasoning processes.

He then goes on to suggest that 'mystical consciousness' belongs to a different but, as it were, parallel order.

As you have already begun to become aware, it is through the operation of the intuition that a new kind of 'knowing' is brought to birth. It is a knowing of that which the intellect and the emotions cannot know by any direct method. It is neither the product of nor a process of reasoning, neither is it brought to birth by heightening of emotional awareness.

This knowing will express itself in great diversity, according to the predisposition, culture and temperament of each individual. For example, Teresa of Avila talks in extravagant terms about 'burning love', 'being drunken with love' and the like. The emotional tones of the mystics in giving expression to their common experience varies all the way from the calm serenity of the Buddha or the German mystic, Meister Eckhart, to the sometimes hyperemotionalism of Teresa. Eckhart expressly rejects hyperemotionalism as part of the mystical experience. He refers to 'storms of emotion' and asserts that they belong to the physical part of our nature, and that the place where the mystical union takes place 'towers high above them'.

What is the core of this knowing? Its central characteristic, as we have already seen, is a dawning awareness of a 'unity', a unity both within myself and within the wider world, i.e., between my total and unified being and all creation. Inherent in this knowing is the dawning of an 'I am' consciousness, a knowledge that I have a right to be, that life on this planet has a place and space which it is my birthright to occupy. Yet this 'I am' consciousness constitutes a paradox, for it is not in the commonly understood sense of the word egocentric. It does not conceive itself to be the centre of all existence but as part of a greater identity, a universal self, embracing all humanity. This has immediate and practical consequences at the level of day-to-day living, for it is then that the intangible manifests and the abstract gives way to the concrete, for the sense of unity gives birth to hope, the ground of all practical virtues.

Mysticism and religion

The question we must now examine is the relationship of mysticism to religion. Traditionally it has been taken for granted by most writers on mysticism that mystical knowledge is a religious experience, religious in the sense that it is bound up with a pattern of dogmatic beliefs. Yet if we are willing to accept Evelyn Underhill's definition (she herself being both a highly respected mystic and a very religious woman) then we see the essential core of mystical consciousness as that of 'union with reality'. Evelyn Underhill, a devout Christian, does not shun the use of the word 'reality' where one might expect her to use the word 'God'! As Stace says in his discourse on the nature of mysticism, 'If we strip the mystical experience of all intellectual interpretation, what is left is simply the undifferentiated unity.'

In the theistic religions of the West, i.e., Christianity, Judaism and Islam, all of which throughout history have at best nurtured and at worst tolerated or persecuted great mystics, the 'knowledge of unity' is interpreted as 'union with God'. What is important to note is that this is an interpretation, it is not the experience of knowledge itself.

Teresa of Avila, who found no incompatability between her orthodox Christian faith and the mystical path, did not have an analytical mind and spoke simple of 'union with God'. The mystics Eckhart and Ruysbroek, the thirteenth-century contempories who may be regarded as more sophisticated than Teresa, wrote and spoke of the undifferentiated unity. Yet as Christian mystics they interpreted this in Trinitarian terms – though one must add that Eckhart was after his death condemned by the Church and declared to have been 'deceived by the Father of Lies'!

The Muslim mystics have interpreted their identical experience in terms of the Unitarian God of Islam. Notable amongst these is the Sufi Ibn Arabi to whom we have already referred. Not only was he a renowned mystic, he was also a highly respected orthodox Muslim theologian. We shall return to Sufism later.

Jewish mysticism appears to fit into a category of its own. Generally speaking it does not speak of union with God, who is always transcendent and 'above' His creation. According to Professor G.G. Scholem the concept of union is alien to Jewish mystical thinking. The earliest Jewish mystics in Talmudic times and later speak of the ascent of the soul to the 'Celestial Throne' where there is the perfect vision of the glory of God. Invariably there is a distance between the soul and God. (See Gershom Scholem, *Major Trends of Jewish Mysticism*, Schocken Books, 1949.) Nevertheless, as in all other religions, the true vision is considered to be non-sensuous.

Perhaps the greatest of all Jewish mystics was Moses, who entered into the 'I AM' consciousness at the burning bush. The story to which we referred in Chapter 1 is recorded in the book of Exodus as follows:

> *Moses was tending the flock of Jethro his father in law . . . and he led the flock to the far side of the desert and came to Horeb the mountain of God. There the angel of the Lord appeared to him in flames of fire from within a bush and though the bush was on fire it did not burn up . . . and God called to him from within the bush, 'Moses, Moses'. And Moses said, 'Here am I' . . . and God said, 'I have come down to deliver my people . . . and now I am sending you to lead them . . . and Moses said, 'How shall I answer them if they say what is the name of this God . . . and God said, 'I AM who I AM'.*

In theological terms and by literal interpretation this was a revelation of Yaweh or I AM to the whole Jewish nation, but at the mystical level it represented a great shift in consciousness on the part of their leader, Moses.

Buddhism, which has produced many mystics, may be regarded in some of its forms as atheistic. It is an open question as to whether in its purest form it is a philosophy rather than a religion. So the essential unity is interpreted as entrance into the void.

India as a nation and Hinduism as a religion have produced

some of the greatest mystics. The realisation of the 'true self' which is also the cosmic or universal self is at the heart of Hindu mysticism. Whilst the mystical path is almost invariably bound up with religious faith and practice, Hinduism is equally ready to recognise that the path of the mystic may be followed in the context of any religion.

Perhaps more than any other individual from within or outside of the world's great religions, Mahatma Gandhi has demonstrated the universal nature of mysticism. Born and raised within Hinduism, Gandhi declared himself to be not only a Hindu but an adherent of all the religions, and showed himself to be equally at home within each one of them. He has been described as 'the universal man'.

Three types of mystic

What becomes clear as we look at some of the great and universal mystics is that they fall into one of three categories. The first is that of those who see themselves as operating within a religious framework with which intellectually they identify, and which they regard as the source and sustenance of their mystical awareness. Into this category we may with certainty place Teresa of Avila and very probably her priest guide and mentor, John of the Cross.

The second category is that of those who, whilst content to remain within the faith system of a particular religion, know themselves and are known to be at home with all religious traditions. Mahatma Gandhi outstandingly represents this.

There is a third category at which we must look. This contains those mystics whose mystical awareness has no primary relationship with religion, yet whose experience is undoubtedly identical to that of those who have lived and moved and had their being within a particular household of faith. I give two examples from the ancient world, teachers whose influence still powerfully affects seekers of the way.

It is to ancient China that we look for such a mystical realisation outside of religion. This is found in Taoism which, loosely interpreted, means 'the way'. According to tradition the founder, Lao Tzu, was born about 570 BC. His teachings are mostly found in his poems. The book containing these poems is called the *Tao Te Ching*. Dr R.B. Blakeney, a translater, in the volume *Lao Tzu* writes: 'The Chinese mystics were original and to the point in their writings, but their point was identical with that of the great mystics elsewhere.' The mystical theme which weaves in and out of the poems may be summed up in those two words, 'the way'.

The following quotations illustrate the Taoist understanding. It will be seen that this is at one with the universal experience. (Both extracts come from *The Way of Life: Tao Te Ching*, by Lao Tzu, translated by R.B. Blakeney and published by New American Library, 1955.)

> *The secret waits for the insight*
> *Of eyes unclouded by longing*
> *Those who are bound by desire*
> *See only the outward container*

This poem echoes something of the Buddhist understanding when it speaks of the void. It has a surprising ending when it suggests a 'predating of God':

> *The way is a void*
> *Used but never filled*
> *An abyss it is*
> *Like an ancestor from which all things come.*

> *It blunts sharpness*
> *Resolves tangles;*
> *It tempers light,*
> *Subdues turmoil.*

A deep pool it is,
Never to run dry!
Whose offspring it may be
I do not know:
It is like a preface to God.

There are many other poems. Together they point 'the way'. To the modern search for a mystical path the Tao has strong appeal.

We turn again to the ancient world for another 'non-religious' mystic. Plotinus was a philosopher who combined great intellectual power with mystical consciousness. He was born in Egypt about AD 205. His mysticism was interpreted not in terms of religion but rather philosophy. He undoubtedly merits a place in the pantheon of 'great mystics', and has been described as 'living proof of the fact that mysticism is not a religious phenomenon'. Here we can refer only briefly to the vast output of Plotinus' teachings. The following quotations indicate his themes. Enlightenment comes not through discursive reasoning. 'For how can,' he asks, 'discursive thought apprehend the absolutely simple?' 'The Light that comes to us as we seek the way comes from the Way and is the One.' He is at one with all the mystics when he says that 'that which excites the keenest longing is without any form, even spiritual form'.

Sufism

Sufism, because of its contemporary appeal to the Western world, requires some special attention. The origin of the word is obscure and is sometimes thought to refer to the long woollen garment worn by some Sufis. Sufis are often equated with and regarded as the mystics of Islam, but scholars and historians are agreed that Sufism predates the Muslim religion. The Sufis merit a special category, for not only do they operate within the context of religions other than Islam, they are able to express their particular ethos outside of a specifically religious context. In his preface to the book *The Sufis* by Idris Shah (Octagon Press, 1964), Robert Graves writes as follows:

> *The Sufis are an ancient spiritual freemasonary whose origins have never been traced or dated . . . though commonly mistaken for Muslim seers the Sufis are at home in all religions . . . According to Ali al Hujwiri, an early authoritative Sufi writer, the prophet Mohammed himself said, 'He who hears the voice of the Sufi people and does not say Amen is recorded in God's presence as one of the heedless.'*

Sufis sometimes call themselves 'the people of the way', i.e., the way of the heart. It is held by many that Francis of Assisi was a Sufi and that a modern Sufi was Pope John XXIII, who in the 1960s threw open the doors of the Roman Catholic Church and called an Ecumenical Council. He was certainly a universal man who could not be contained exclusively in the religion of which he was the head.

Sufis make much of the levels of understanding in relation to the Qur'an in particular and sacred scriptures in general. These levels range from literal interpretation to the purely mystical. There are many Sufi Orders throughout the world, each having its own particular ethos. Music, dance (i.e., the Whirling Dervishes) and parabolic teaching are central to the Sufi path. The parables they tell can themselves be heard at different levels. Often they are very humorous but none the less profound in their wisdom. The Nasruddin stories have done much to spread Sufism in the West in the second half of this century. Nasruddin is a fictional folk hero. The following story has to do with the nature of truth and may be seen as pivotal to Sufi understanding:

Nasruddin in debate with a certain King asserted that laws as such could not make better people. The King disagreed and said that he could and would force people to observe and obey the truth. Guards were stationed nearby the city entrance. All who wished to enter would be questioned. 'Those who answer truthfully will be allowed to enter,' said the King. 'Others will be beheaded.' Nasruddin immediately presented himself at the gate and was challenged by the guard and asked where he was going. Nasruddin replied confidently, 'I am on my way to be beheaded.' The guard replied that he did not believe him. 'In that case,' said Nasruddin, 'behead me.' 'But if we do that,' said the guard, 'and hang you for lying we shall have made what you said come true.' 'Precisely,' said Nasruddin. 'Now you know what truth is . . . YOUR TRUTH.'

Characteristic of the Sufis is their intense awareness of God indwelling, not only within human beings but within all Creation. For this reason the great monotheistic religions with their emphasis upon the otherness of God have often regarded the Sufis with suspicion. Frequently they have been dismissed as heretics. Abu Yazid al Bistani, who died in 875 having declared that God dwelt within him, horrified the orthodox by exclaiming, 'Glory to me, how great is my majesty.' Another Sufi mystic Al Hallaj was crucified in 922 for using language which to the orthodox implied that he was claiming to be a divine incarnation. So deeply was he conscious of the 'I AM' identity that he proclaimed 'I am the Truth'. Here we have a powerful echo of the often misunderstood words of Jesus Christ: 'I am the way, the truth and the life. . .'

Mystical awareness

It is this 'I am' consciousness which figures so prominently in today's mystical awareness, an awareness expressing itself in great diversity of forms. I give two examples from my own experience. The first of these concerned the elderly Abbess whose encounter in the orchard so opened the eyes of her heart.

In her eighties, with the simplicity of a little child, she began to practise a daily meditation which involved a centring in the heart and a repetition of the mantric words 'I am'. With a sensitivity born of many years of single-pointedness and humility she rapidly became aware of what Evelyn Underhill describes as the 'union with reality'. That reality was for her the Christ whose faithful servant she had striven to be throughout her long life. So profound was this change of consciousness that she began to feel 'possessed by Christ'. Fearful that what she was experiencing did not conform to her totally orthodox Christian faith she sent an urgent message that I should visit her. Sitting in her cell, her frail old body trembling from head to foot, she whispered, 'What is happening to me? For during my times of meditation I hear my heart repeating the words "I am Christ".' I was able to reassure her that this had been the common experience of some of the Church's great mystics down through the ages and that she was not a heretic!

The second example is very different yet essentially the same. A young man, Peter, in his mid-thirties, having been happily married for five years was suddenly widowed, losing both his wife and two children in a car accident. Everything which gave meaning to his life was suddenly taken from him. For twelve months he struggled to maintain his sanity. Having been brought up in an atheistic family, religion and what it offered had no meaning for him. Eventually, persuaded by a friend to investigate a yoga class, he found himself almost against his will deciding to join.

Supported by his friend he doggedly persisted week after week until, after six months, just when he was about to give up the practice, something dramatic happened. He described this as follows: 'For six months I had practised the discipline of yoga, for most of the time regarding it as something to fill the awful gap in my life with a probable body benefit. Then quite suddenly things began to change. I realised that the disciplines I had been following were creating what I can only describe as a new space in my life. Until then all I was conscious of was pain and loss. Now I was aware of a new "me" coming to birth, a "me" that in some mysterious way was no longer obliterated by suffering and self-pity. This new identity or (as I now see it) my true identity was conscious of being linked to something sustaining, something which gave me hope. I had begun to discover who I was and what I was for.'

How different was the language of Peter from that of the Lady Abbess, and how far apart their experiences of life. Yet both were on the same path of self-discovery. The worlds which they inhabited appear to be poles apart, yet the fruits of their commitment are one and the same. Both discovered their lives opening to a new reality. Consciousness now for both of them centred in the universal self. The Abbess knew it to be 'the Christ'. Peter knew it to be the 'Source'. For each it was both intensely personal yet universal. Personal because it gave them a profound sense of personhood, and universal because it was the realisation not only of a union with divinity, but also with all created things.

Towards universal spirituality

In 1993 I took part in the centenary celebrations in India of the *World Congress of Faiths*. Founded in 1893, this constituted a courageous pioneer movement to bring the world's main religions into the experience of at least mutual respect and peaceful co-existence. Few at that time could have foreseen that over the years sights would be raised and vision enlarged to embrace aspirations towards a universal spirituality.

At the centenary celebrations this was the dominant chord struck by speakers representing many faiths and cultures. Many times the question was raised, 'Is there a path of unity to be followed which does not require us to deny the reality of our very diverse and often apparently contradictory statements of faith?'

I was particularly intrigued by the response of a young South Indian to this question: 'Can we not see the whole pattern as that of a wheel? The hub represents the sharing of a common experience of God . . . the experience we have shared at a very deep level as we have been silent together in this conference . . ., the spokes leading outwards are the different ways of expressing this experience. The circle or rim of the wheel represents the binding together of the whole. This conference gathering is a binding together. Let us follow the spokes back to the centre where true unity is to be found.'

After the gathering I asked the young man to tell me about his own experience of this unity. He introduced himself as a Christian priest. 'My spiritual roots are in the Christian tradition,' he explained, 'but not in any exclusive interpretation of that faith, for I am committed to the realising of a universal spirituality. I see the great faith events of Christ's life as powerful mirror images of the spiritual journey which all of us must take if we are to fulfil our destiny. In the use of language familiar to all Indians I see the fact of Christ's death as uniquely demonstrating the truth at the heart of all religions, i.e., that the ego must die if we are to find resurrection.'

We have seen so far that the great characteristic of the mystical path is 'union'. Inherent in this sense of oneness is not only an assurance of meaning and purpose but also that of being held within an unchanging and unconditional love. Whether this love is conceived of as the love of a Creator Parent God or whether the Reality at the heart of the Universe is of secondary significance, union in the context of meaning and purpose would be a contradiction in terms without love.

We now pose the question, 'Is the experience of the awakened heart leading to the mystical path open to all?' Seen as 'the art of union with reality' and 'experiential wisdom', I would answer an unequivocal 'yes'. The expressions and articulations of this experience will be as varied as are human beings. The door will be opened to all who knock.

MEDITATION EXERCISE

We need now to bring our perception of 'mystical consciousness' into a meditative exercise. This involves, as before, a conscious use of your capacity to Reflect, and also to use your Imagination and to develop your capacity for Intuition.

REFLECTION

We have considered some of the varieties of expression given to a common God-given experience. To reflect upon this brings us to a pin-pointing of the essence of this experience and a recognition not only of the validity but the inevitability of diverse interpretations.

The essence of this experience we have defined as 'light'. The light is a symbol and sign which speaks to the heart of the human condition. As a symbol it resonates at once with the desire to know, for it symbolises the knowing described as we have seen in Browning's 'Paracelsus'. As a sign it confirms the Divine presence. So we both know the Divine power and our knowledge is confirmed by the light. We are sharing in an illumination, claiming as our very birthright what has been described as 'the light that lightens everyone'.

IMAGINATION

We may bring this concept of light to the centre of our creative imagination as we continue on our pilgrimage: the path from the open heart lies straight ahead, a ribbon of light leading to distant horizons as yet but dimly perceived. I am aware of an impulse within and a kind of beckoning from far ahead, both of which not only urge me onward but also sustain me in this. Movement forward brings further clarity of vision and I now see on either side of the way ahead houses of many shapes and sizes. These I recognise as households of faith. Some have many windows, others only a few. From these windows light is streaming down on to the path. I also perceive that there are houses joined together by bridges which cross over the highway. In spite of the comfort and reassurance which comes from these houses, I know that in order to proceed with single-mindedness along this path I must travel onwards. I am grateful for the fact that many of them offer safe and secure lodging. I am aware also that many travellers on the way, dedicated seekers, are finding in these houses refreshment and restoration. All this encourages and strengthens me as I press ahead.

INTUITION

In moving from reflection and the use of our creative imagination we go systematically through the relaxation exercise we have learned and go through the process of body-consciousness (See Chapter 2).

From this we move to a focussing within the heart and become aware of the light within. We allow the light to fill the body and to be conscious of the fact that 'My physical body is permeated with the Divine Light'. I know also that at the level of the heart I am linked to all the people of the way. Together we form a vast network of light, and I rest in this truth.

I close and confirm my meditation with the words:

> *The light shines on in the darkness*
> *And the darkness can never overcome it.*

5

The Way of the Contemplative

Contemplation unites us with God at a vertical level where
we transcend ourselves, the world and all our problems, and
experience oneness with God. It is at the same time a mode
of action at the horizontal level by which we go out from the
centre of peace . . . to the whole world. The further we go
vertically towards God the further we can go horizontally
towards men. Jesus was totally surrendered to the vertical
movement and totally open to people and life as a whole.

DOM BEDE GRIFFITHS, *The Universal Christ*
(Darton, Longman and Todd, 1990)

The journey 'into God' is concerned with life as a whole. It is
not an adding on to everyday living. Rather it is a taking up of
every aspect of your life, giving life and purpose to the humdrum, the routine, the understood and the puzzling.

You now have your feet firmly planted on what the mystics
have called the contemplative path. We shall look carefully at
the meaning of the word later but before that we need to pause
mentally, to step back from the acquisition of further information and to look at this mystical consciousness in the context of
our experience of life so far.

No human being is exempt from life's perturbations.
Achievement and disappointment, pain and suffering and also fulfilment and joy are our common lot. In this chapter we shall look
at how your experience of life so far can be related to the journey.

Stages of discernment

In the diversities of experience which precede finding the contemplative way two distinct stages may frequently be discerned, the one giving birth to the other. Both of these stages may also reassert themselves, even when we have begun to move with assurance into the realm of experiential wisdom. It is therefore important that we are aware of these differing levels of human consciousness.

These states or stages, like mysticism, may operate either within or outside of a religious context, or contain both secular and religious elements. The manner of their expression will therefore take a variety of shapes, expressing themselves in a diversity of ways. In essence they are the same.

The first stage is that of the 'conventional' or the mechanical following of a particular behaviour pattern. Such a pattern may have outgrown social, cultural and 'spiritual' strands. These may be inherited or formed from our own long-established lifestyle. How do they come into being and what are the factors which establish them?

These patterns may arise from the crystallising of what was initially a creative energy operating within the life experience. This energy at a given point and in relation to a specific need functioned in a particular and possibly unique manner. The unconsciously repeated and automatic reproduction of this pattern, regardless of changing circumstances and fresh needs, produces stereotyped behaviour, often completely divorced from the immediate need and therefore inappropriate to new situations. The past is thus imposed upon the present, stifling new movement and growth in perception.

There is a story from the East which tells of a revered guru who was undoubtedly a man of great spiritual stature. Daily he gave audience to large numbers of his devoted followers. Each morning the guru would enter the audience hall accompanied by his favourite cat. Before being seated he would place the cat on a cushion where it remained throughout the audience. This continued for many years until the guru died. The cat remained and daily was placed on the same cushion by the side of the guru's empty chair. In the fullness of time the cat also died. The guru was regarded as irreplaceable but a new cat was seen to be indispensable, for by this time the cat, the cushion and the empty chair had become necessary objects of devotion. It is said that today in many places the successors of the original disciples still culti-vate the cult of the cat, the cushion and the chair. The dynamic which had once operated so effectively through the guru had crystallised into a 'spiritual' convention!

Breaking down conventions

How may such conventions be broken down? When firmly established and forming deeply rooted behaviour patterns, shock, i.e., the experience of being brought face to face with one's condition and the reality of the situation, may be neces-sary to release the dynamic from the crystallised form. This can operate both within a group or with individuals. In a group sit-uation effective shock may take place as a result of conscious releasing of the dynamic by a discerning facilitator, i.e., one who perceives the need and the capacity of members of the group to respond. The same may happen in a one-to-one situ-ation between a sufficiently aware spiritual guide and his or her disciple. When a sufficient self-awareness has been developed and where self-observation is practised as a discipline, shock may be self-administered.

For the majority, 'shock therapy' comes about through the life crises to which all humans are subjected, for example sud-den illness or bereavement. Such shocks may be seen and indeed claimed as opportunities for release from imprisoning conventions.

The perspectives we are learning to take on this journey can be the means not of minimising the effects of shock but of helping us to experience, even through suffering and perplexity, a greater good.

Even an apparently genuine search for spiritual enlightenment may represent a conventional mind-set rather than a single-pointed desire that real need should be met.

A young man from the West convinced himself that above all things he wanted spiritual enlightenment. He was hazy as to what this meant but was quite sure that this was what he needed for his true well-being. Upon arriving in north India in order to pursue his search, to his delight he came across a travelling *sadhu* or holy man reputed to have the power to bestow enlightenment. Without invitation the young man attached himself to the spiritual master and for many days followed him, travelling from village to village pleading to be shown the secret of enlightenment. Never once did the object of his repeated enquiry either speak to him or give any indication that he was aware of his presence until one day they arrived at the bank of a river. Turning to the would-be disciple the teacher beckoned him to follow. When both were waist deep in the water he suddenly plunged the young man head first into the river and in spite of his struggles held him there for five seconds. Grasping for breath he struggled to the surface to hear the *sadhu* speak for the first time, 'When you cease to behave like a parrot and want enlightenment as much as you just now wanted air, you will find it.'

Charismatic energy

With the breakdown of stereotyped behaviour patterns and conditioned responses the immediate result is the creation of a vacuum. The human being, like the whole of nature, 'abhors a vacuum'. As a result this vacuum within the mental and emotional fields receives an influx of potentially creative energy. Frequently there follows a dramatic thrusting into a stage of potential transition and supernormal energy levels are achieved.

This we may describe as the 'charismatic' stage or second stage. A fixed and frequently paralysing situation has been dramatically changed into one of fluidity. An unpredictable power potential has been created.

When this takes place in a group and when those involved are concerned with ethical or spiritual values this new energy may be consciously channelled, and the impact may determine a whole new direction for life.

Some definition of the word charismatic is necessary. The word itself is derived from the Greek *charisma*, signifying a supernormal power. In common parlence it is used to describe individuals who at the level of personality evidence a particularly powerful magnetism.

Since the 1960s a great deal of supernormal or charismatic energy has been released into Western society. Many factors have contributed to this development. The old secular and religious stereotypes have been challenged. Shocks have been administered to ancient institutions. Conventions have been challenged and patent hypocrises brought into the light. Cultic forms have been undermined and crystallised dynamics released.

The state of flux, this charismatic stage within which Western society still finds itself, has yet to find the means by which these new energies can be transmuted, directed and used creatively.

Within the Christian Church a movement which came to be known as the Charismatic Revival came to birth in the transition period of the 1960s. This movement has acted as a catalyst for a great manifestation of energy in churches which for centuries had been locked within stereotyped forms. Over a very wide spectrum religious conventions have been shocked into oblivion. The movement has been characterised by a great proliferation of psychic gifts. Hitherto subservient and conventional congregations have experienced great explosions of energy. Understood to be 'gifts of the Spirit', powers of healing, speaking in tongues, clairvoyance and clairaudience have characterised the movement.

The dramatic effects of this movement within the ecclesiastical structures is evidenced by the great changes which have taken place in many church interiors. Wooden pews which for centuries had encased generations of the faithful have been swept away. Space has been created for movement and dance. Previously captive audiences have been caught up in spontaneous and sometimes unrestrained activity. Pulpits which have for long elevated the clergy to 'six feet above criticism' have become obsolete as the faithful have themselves become teachers of the faith. Buildings for worship have metaphorically been turned inside out as congregations have asserted that the people themselves are the Church.

The break with centuries of conventionalism has undoubtedly achieved a great deal. The weakness of the movement lies in the fact that frequently it has failed to perceive itself to be in a stage of transition and as a result has turned introspectively in upon itself. When the incapacity to maintain a high emotional pitch has become evident, guilt and an unreal sense of failure has followed.

Various 'New Age' groups have effected similar results from the use of shock techniques. The Findhorn Community, to which we have already referred, has pioneered the way in this field, organising a great variety of courses bringing thousands of young people into experiential situations designed to release creativity. This has undoubtedly enabled many from a great variety of backgrounds to sever inhibiting links with convention-ridden pasts.

Claiming the results of shock

In the context of the pilgrimage we have undertaken our concern is particularly with what I have referred to as 'claiming the results of shock', and how the stage of charismatic release and transition may be channelled. For it is uniquely given to human beings not only positively to sustain shock but also to turn its effects into a new and creative energy which may be consciously shaped and directed.

It is said that the godson of Coleridge, the poet, when told that he had less than a year to live, replied: 'Then tomorrow I must begin to learn Sanskrit.' For him the transition stage, the release of supernormal power resulting from shock, led immediately to the opening of new horizons of productivity.

The wife of a close friend was tragically widowed at a very early age. She grieved deeply, for the couple had been much in love. Their marriage had followed a conventional pattern and within that framework life had been contented if unremarkable. Within a year of her bereavement she was able to move forward on the very wings of grief to something new. 'I have begun to realise,' she confided, 'that I can as an artist now give myself to a creativity that I could never have achieved before.' Here was no disloyalty but a movement towards new horizons. From a happy marriage dramatically ended she had moved through shock to glimpse and give herself to the release of new creative activity.

In both these instances the stage of transition was rapid. The release and transmuting of energy followed quickly upon the breakdown of previous patterns.

Very different in the pattern it followed, but identical in end results, was the case of a woman who described herself to me as emotionally paralysed. Timid by nature, in her late thirties and following years of trauma as a result of 'forgotten' child abuse, she had plucked up enough courage to undergo psychotherapy. Through skilful therapy she had recalled what was undoubtedly the origin of her emotional paralysis. An initial deep sense of healing followed. Too quickly she withdrew from professional help and, through lack of further support and in spite of her religious faith, she became increasingly bitter against the perpetrator of the abuse. Heart and mind became firmly closed. She began to cosset the wound within and took refuge in the confines of a closed Fundamentalistic group, cocooning herself into judgemental isolation.

The crystallised state within which she was encased was eventually broken and healing energy released. This was brought about by the regular practice of gentle meditative exercises. The transition took time and the process was not without pain. The fulfilment was the opening of the heart and a conscious following of the contemplative path.

What is this way and how may it be followed and developed? To contemplate is to see into things as they really are. It is a looking into reality. Yet this is very much more than a passive observation. It is linked to what Coleridge's godson saw immediately as new horizons of possibility and the widow experienced as a new creative energy. It is both the seeing and the experiencing of new possibilities; it is the beholding of an open door and an entering in to a new world of unrealised potential.

Contemplation and self-awareness

We may carry this a stage further as we see this experience of contemplation to consist of the opening up of a channel between the observer and what is observed. The release of the woman I have described as for long existing in a 'crystallised state' led on to the experience of first of all becoming aware of another learning to 'contemplate God'. That this was no fanciful illusion was attested by the integrated life which stemmed from this experience. She was consciously directing the energies of release. Contemplation became for her not a thinking about Divine nature, nor an attempt to analyse exactly the Divine attributes, but rather to be aware of the God reality, to look into God. A channel was opened up and a new and creative energy began to flow into her life. The practice of contemplative meditation brought release and creativity together.

From this it will be seen that to look contemplatively is not to analyse. It is to behold not with the senses but with the eyes of the heart, an awareness which takes us beyond sensual perception. There is no area of life, no aspect of creation to which this way of seeing does not apply. We shall see this as we pursue our journey. At the very centre of contemplative life is the practice of self-observation, a practice you are developing through meditation.

To observe myself in this manner is something quite distinct from self-analysis, which is a mental activity. Neither is it introspection, which is emotional involvement with myself. Self-observation proceeds from the capacity to stand back and to see within myself possibility, potential and the opening of doors towards new horizons.

As we travel along the contemplative path we also develop the capacity to see into other people, and this without intrusion or judgement, a seeing which is also the opening up of a channel for the flow of creative energy. It is seeing which is also a giving.

So do I begin to understand that reality is much more than that perceived by the five senses. To sensible perception this is a mystery. Yet its results are essentially practical. It is the basis of all self-knowledge, an accurate understanding of others and the laying of foundations for a contemplative philosophy of life.

Contemplative meditation

We shall encounter these areas of contemplative awareness as we pursue our journey. We need now to examine the central means by which contemplative awareness is fostered and developed – the practice of contemplative meditation.

The word meditation came suddenly into Western consciouness and into the popular vocabulary of those on a spiritual path in the 1960s and 1970s. The great dislocation of spirituality from formal religion required a new vocabulary to describe eternal realities. The God of the churches had suffered widespread rejection, and with that rejection the concept of prayer quickly evaporated. Prayer had to be addressed to a person. It required an object to which it could be directed. It presupposed theological concepts, divine images and symbols. All this was consigned to history and dismissed with the demise of religion. Meditation required no such definition of Divinity and fitted very well into the climate of theological agnosticism.

We need now to look at its relationship to the contemplative path. Meditation comprehends three distinct aspects of the human's total being: the intellect, the imagination and the intuition.

When the first of these is put into operation then the activity involved is described as reflective. When the imagination is employed the process is creative. With the bringing into operation of the intuitive faculty then meditation becomes contemplative. So we may speak of three distinct practices which qualify the word meditation – reflective meditation, creative meditation and that which particularly concerns us, i.e., contemplative meditation.

Until the general severence of spirituality from religion, apart from the experience of the mystics and the practice of contemplative religious communities, meditation was in the Western tradition equated almost exclusively with the activity of the intellect, reinforced by that of the imagination.

I recall as a theological student being advised by my Spiritual Director to spend half an hour each morning meditating on a passage of Scripture. I determined to excel in the practice. Entering the chapel I ascetically chose (as I supposed for the good of my soul) the place which would give the maximum bodily discomfort. Wedged in between narrow wooden pews I lowered myself on to the narrow kneeling strip provided. The passage I had been given upon which to meditate (i.e., think about) was the story of Jesus of Nazareth walking on the water and His call to His disciple Peter to join Him. 'Use your imagination well,' my director had advised. I did and immediately conjured up lurid images of the two characters. Struggle as I could, everything went wrong. First I had a vivid picture of Jesus sinking, then Peter swam towards Him. Finally I found myself taking charge of the boat (no doubt a significant factor). The reflective stage was no more successful. It only carried my imagination into further fantasies. Isolated from a conscious centring in the heart – beyond thought – the experience became one of riding on an intellectual roundabout! All this was far removed from contemplative meditation.

In later years, having well begun the practice of contemplative meditation, I was able to turn again from time to time with a quieter mind to reflection.

STEPS INTO CONTEMPLATION

So what practical and experiential steps can we take in learning to practise contemplative meditation? Here we shall look at what may be regarded as the essential ingredients and the pattern as a whole. At the end of the chapter we shall build upon the simple preparatory exercises given in the two previous chapters.

THE BODY

It is of fundamental importance that the significance of the physical body is given full recognition. For too long many religious traditions have denigrated its significance. Asceticism has taken extreme forms, and the body has been seen as a hindrance to the spiritual path. The physical body is the focal point in time and space for the realisation of a potential which at this stage of human evolution we can but dimly perceive. The very first step in moving towards a meditative exercise is the recognition and reverencing of my body. I recognise it as uniquely mine; a pattern of energies which has no exact counterpart anywhere else in the physical world. It holds all the possibilities of the present moment and presages all future development.

My body is the outward and visible expression of my

Essence (soul), it is through my body the Essence is ever urging me onwards towards an ultimate fulfilment beyond time and space. This is a great mystery which reveals itself to consciousness as I give place, space and proper recognition to this physical aspect of my total being.

From this arises the question of how do you prepare your body consciously to meditate?

In the 1960s and 1970s 'meditation stools' were regarded as *de rigueur* for all would-be meditators. At that time influences from the East were at their height and the way of the Easterner was either to sit cross-legged upon the floor or to squat on a special stool with the legs tucked underneath. For most Westerners this is neither natural nor comfortable. The only important factor is to be able to be comfortable and potentially relaxed, and to move on from body-consciousness.

THE BREATH

It is very easy to give a pseudo-mystical significance to the breath on the one hand and on the other to ignore it completely. The breath is an expression of the life force by which we live and move and have our being. It represents in and through the physical form the Divine creative activity, that movement which out of the void brought all Creation into being and which is ever renewing, recreating and bringing back to source. As with the mystery of the physical body so the mystery of the breath has an immediate and practical application. My inbreathing is a receiving and my outbreath a sharing. The very first step in breath consciousness is to go with it in a process of relaxation. There should be no unnatural nor artificial controlling of the breath. Your natural breathing rhythm is sufficient to fulfil its highest function. To that natural rhythm we relate the releasing of body tension. At a later stage we may see the breath as conveying all that is contained in the words 'Communion with God'.

INTELLECT

For many of us for much of the time the intellect exercises a tyrannical power. It has been said that rarely does a human being think from his or her self and that almost all thinking is the result of external stimuli, impressions received from beyond ourselves. So chains of thought are broken into, thinking goes round in circles, gives way to fresh impressions from new circumstances or evaporates altogether.

The intellect like the body requires full recognition. It is not to be rejected nor is it to be suppressed. Indeed the impossibility of this is evidenced by what happens if I am ordered, for example, 'not to think of a pink elephant'. The immediate response of the intellect is to think of precisely that! It requires a place to rest, a point upon which to focus. Learning to do this can be achieved by stages. For example, my intellect awareness may be focussed upon my body, i.e., not to think *about* the body but to be body-*conscious*. To do this whilst holding a picture of my body in my mind's eye can bring a powerful and precious moment of mind stillness and I am learning to observe myself without Self-analysis.

EMOTIONS

As with the intellect, the emotions can, and for many of us frequently do, exercise a controlling power. Such control is never lessened by repression, for to pretend that they do not exist is to batten down the hatches and to create a potentially dangerous and destructive situation. It is therefore important that in meditation I give full recognition to the fact that they are part of the totality of my being. I do not judge them as either good or bad. I acknowledge them. 'I have emotions but I am not my emotions' articulates the reality which, if treated gently, they will acknowledge. In the process of stepping back from my emotions the controlling ties are loosened and I am learning to observe myself without introspection.

CENTRING

'To centre' is a universally accepted description of bringing the whole of my person into an integrated harmony. Yet the question must be asked 'centring where?' So far we have seen the human being – I have seen myself – as constituting Body, Intellect and Emotions. These two capacities to think and to feel may be related to 'centres' in the body; to think is the capacity of the brain, to feel reactionally we relate to the solar plexus. The pivot of balance, the place in which the energies represented by thought and feeling may be transmuted and directed, is 'the heart'. This is the place of true centring.

By nature the human being is controlled and directed, as we have seen, by the combined forces of thought and emotion. As part of what we may see as a tripartite human being they are unable of themselves to act in harmony. Their full potential cannot be exploited.

Any meditative practice which fails to recognise this fact will also fail to establish a link with the Source or God, from which all life derives its origins, by which it is sustained and to which ultimately it must return. A supposed harmony which seeks to operate in isolation from the Source may acquire a semblance of well-being. It is nevertheless cut off from its source of true fulfilment.

It is here that we remind ourselves of the purpose of meditation. This is union with the Source or God. The techniques which I practise in order to effect this are means to an end, never ends in themselves. There is nothing magical nor even sacred about them. We use them because they have been well and truly tried by the 'people of the way'.

Remember that centring in the heart is a kind of entering into the void, for here we let go of sensation and verbalisation. In the early stages of practising meditation it is very easy to become trapped into the wrong kind of expectation. Sensations are sought and feelings are 'tested'. It is in the not knowing that heart-knowledge is developed. The void, as we have seen, is that state of consciousness beyond reflection and beyond the imagination. And it is from within the void that a creative life force is born.

Creation stories embodied in many religious and cultured traditions articulate this reality in mythical form. In the book called Genesis, 'The Book of Beginnings,' we read 'Now the earth was without form and void . . . and God said let there be light . . .' and from this light all things took their form. So as I link with the Light I become part of the ongoing Divine creativity.

THE LIGHT

The concept of light is central to all our meditational exercises. As reflection of the Divine presence its history is both ancient and universal. It is probably the only image of God acceptable to all religions. It transcends all barriers and boundaries established by the diversities of creeds and dogmas. Throughout history in legends and in myth and in Sacred writings 'beings of light' have been harbingers of the Deity's presence. Light is seen to dispel darkness. The forces of Light are seen to overcome the powers of darkness. The blessed enter into eternal Light whilst the damned are cast into outer darkness. In short light is equated with the Divine whilst darkness signifies the demonic. So deeply is this imprinted upon the consciousness of certain ethnic groups that the sun itself is held to be the authentic face of the Divine. The cycle of its appearance at the dawning of each new day has etched into the human psyche, light as the herald of new birth, sustenance and transformation.

Thus life-giving light is reflected in the descriptions given to men and women whose lives have demonstrated qualities recognised as superhuman or Divine. Such people are described as 'children of the Light'.

The presence of all great spiritual leaders and teachers has been seen as synonymous with the light.

Of Gautama the Buddha it has been said that his disciples at times had to divert their gaze to avoid being blinded by the light which radiated from him. The prophet Moses, on descending from Mount Sinai where he had received the Ten Commandments from Yahweh, had to veil his face from the people because of the brilliance of the light reflected there.

Jesus Christ, described as the 'Light of the World', was transfigured, i.e., transmuted into light in the presence of three of his disciples. The prophet Muhammad was seen as 'the light of Allah on earth'.

Throughout history the saints of all religious traditions have been depicted in art as surrounded by light. So we in our meditational exercises enter into this one unified and unifying light.

LENGTH OF TIME

Here there can be no clear-cut answer to the question of how long should each exercise last. What can be said with certainty is that the length of time is of no primary importance. Five minutes may hold as much significance as an hour. To practise this daily can change the whole direction of my life. And remember that meditation is a means to an end, never an end in itself. A great spiritual teacher was asked by an enthusiastic disciple, 'For how many hours daily should I meditate?' The teacher replied, 'If you make a fetish of meditation God will make you give it up!'

MEDITATION EXERCISE

REFLECTION

The way of the contemplative is the path of opportunity. To travel in that way is to move out of all forms of stagnation, mental and emotional. Gradually the chains of convention can be broken and unresolved energies directed towards a clear aim. I bring with me every part of my being, for all has meaning. Visions of a clear and purposeful way of living open before me. Past frustrations and sorrows can generate energies of creativity. Every day brings a fresh beginning, a letting go of the past and a commitment to the way.

IMAGINATION

In my mind's eye I see the road ahead. It is well made and though it rises and falls, dipping into valleys and ascending again, it is very straight, leading far beyond my present sight. Above the sky is cloudless, giving clarity to the picture. My feet are firmly planted on the path and I am ready to move.

CONTEMPLATION

Without haste I move through the stages of relaxation.
Centring in the heart I am aware of the light within.
The light is also a stillness.
The light permeates my whole being and is ever renewed by my breathing.
I give myself to the stillness.

I affirm and confirm my meditation with the words:

In your light shall we see light

6

The How of Learning

Do not build up your views upon your senses and your thoughts, do not base your understanding upon your senses and your thoughts; but at the same time do not seek the mind away from your senses and thoughts, do not try to grasp reality by rejecting your senses and thoughts. When you are neither attached to, nor detached from them, then you enjoy your perfect unconstructed freedom, then you have your seat of enlightenment.

ZEN MASTER HUANG-PO

The path along which you are travelling is concerned above all else with the business of living. Progress is proven by the steadily growing ability to face life in all its dimensions and to realise within ourselves the capacity to see meaning and purpose in the world of which we are a part.

The regular practice of contemplative meditation will provide you with the foundation for the building of a kind of watch-tower, a vantage point from which you can look from a new perspective at all life. A learning process has begun. Now you need to foster this widening vision, through wisdom and knowing rather than education.

For most of us the word 'education' is invested with one meaning and one only, i.e., the grasping of ideas by the intellect. This is the underlying philosophy of the accepted systems of education, both secular and religious, in the Western world today. The gain, if such it can be called, from this concept of education is that the educated, the ones who are supposed to know, are in effect continually expanding encyclopedias. The loss, and it is a heavy one, is that the information acquired is all too often totally divorced from the business of living. Such knowledge is far removed from wisdom. It is isolated, barren and uncreative, shut in within the confines of its own limitations.

Shakespeare describes such a state in *The Merchant of Venice* (I, ii, 13):

> *If to do were as easy as to know what were good to do, chapels had been churches, and poor men's cottages princes' palaces. It is a good divine that follows his own instructions; I can easier teach twenty what were good to be done than be one of the twenty to follow mine own teaching. The brain may devise laws for the blood, but a hot temper leaps o'er a cold decree; such a hare is madness the youth, to skip o'er the meshes of good counsel the cripple.*

The hollowness of an educational system which confines its attention to the human capacity to assimilate information was poignantly illustrated for me by the *cri de coeur* of a religiously educated woman who came to me for help. Both she and her husband were active members of what they described as a 'lively' spiritual group. My first contact with her took place shortly after she had been diagnosed as suffering from an incurable disease. 'It is probable,' she said, 'that I am soon going to die. Throughout my life I have belonged to a "believing community". I have struggled to follow all its precepts. I have read the right books and studied the Scriptures but somehow there is a reservoir of truth in my head from which the real me is blocked off. Tell me what I must do?' Here was the will and the desire to know, but neither study nor devotion had enabled her to effect the bridging of the gap between theory and practice. Her response to the practice of meditation was dramatic and the last months of her life witnessed to a deep and transforming peace.

The beginning of true learning is to know that divorced from response on a level other than the intellect, the amassing of facts, however edifying, creates barriers against true learning. It is to know that definitions and concepts, however excellent, if unrelated to what we have discovered to be the primary level of perception amount to the adding of no more than interesting, albeit 'spiritual', supplements to existing encyclopedias.

Such learning does not come easily, for the focussing of our attention upon something other than the grasping of ideas involves cutting across what for many of us are deeply ingrained habits. It means the conscious and progressive disruption of long-established thought patterns and the recognition and control of automatic responses. Our ability to do this grows from the regular practice of self-observation.

Harmony

The power of sound to break through the conditioned mind-set and to produce harmony within the human being is long forgotten in the Western religious tradition. Here we should remind ourselves that harmony within the total being is something quite different from what is generally thought of as harmony in music. The dissonance of a Stockhausen or a Stravinsky has much greater potency for promoting change within the hearer than the popular 'harmonies' produced by the great romantic composers. For it is when music breaks through and cuts across soporific patterns that a creative resonance is produced.

In the book *All and Everything: Meetings with Remarkable Men* George Ivanovitch Gurdjieff describes a festival of music held annually in a remote part of Afghanistan. Musicians and singers converged in a particular valley. There they would enter a competition. This was of a very unusual kind. It was not primarily to do with musical skill, but rather with the capacity through music and sound to set up a resonance between voice and instrument and the surrounding rocks and mountains. One after another would compete until it suddenly happened. The mountains became alive. A remarkable vibrational response had been called forth. The whole valley became part of and echoed back the sound effecting a sense of harmony beyond description.

In a much less exotic situation – the large lounge of a Tunbridge Wells hotel – I myself took part in a similar experience. The event was described as 'A Day of Renewal through Sound'. All taking part were at a certain point invited to 'sound your own note' and to do this without any attempt to 'harmonise'. Within minutes the walls, the ceiling and even the furnishings were singing back.

Such events have a releasing effect. They are not an imposition upon the emotions and, like all valid spiritual experiences, they lead beyond themselves. They lead to the evoking of silent music within the depths of one's being, an intuitive unarticulated knowing, a sharing in the unity of all creation – a sharing which we may find difficult to articulate but which is part of our deep knowing.

Although, as I have indicated, the West has neglected this powerful means of awakening and learning, both Jewish and Christian traditions use words of power frequently in their forms of worship. The long 'a' i.e., the *aa* sound vibrates powerfully with what we have described as the heart centre. So 'Amen', 'Alleluia', and the Aramaic 'Maranatha', ('Come, Lord), can – when sounded upon a single note, unembellished with florid music – call to the very depth of our being.

During a visit to a church in New Zealand I was emboldened in a very traditional setting to use sound in the place of meeting what I have called a 'singing and sermon expectancy'. Entering the pulpit I began with the usual preparatory prayer, and followed this not with the expected sermon but the repetition of the word Amen to chant. In my judgement the long silence which followed was far more eloquent than any verbal exhortation which I could have made.

An exception to the discarding of the use of sound in the

Western tradition is the singing of plainsong, chiefly kept alive by the monastic houses of the Roman Catholic and Anglican Churches. At its best such chanting is egoless and therefore heart-centred, for individual personalities are excluded from its corporate expression. At the end of this century we are witnessing a revival of plainchant in an unexpected area, for it is becoming a part of pop culture and has even reached the top of the charts!

Idealism and aspirations

The last quarter of the twentieth century has witnessed the emergence of many new spiritual impulses in society. Because of the failure to initiate and to understand the process of true learning focussed through the practice of meditation, the churches have frequently failed to foster these new impulses. As a result idealism has far outstripped human capacity to respond. So we see the great human contradiction manifesting. Noble sentiments and ideals are born. These blossom and at the same time run parallel to an increased generation of aggressive and reactionary energies, which could with knowledge be channelled into a new creativity.

The confusion is heightened as we see campaigns for human rights, animal rights, ecological and many other 'rights' gaining impetus on those very energies which they set out to demolish. In the name of peace aggression is released and focussed upon those who are seen to be its enemies. In defence of animal rights the reactionary animal urge to defend and even destroy frequently controls the behaviour of these defenders, and in the effort to preserve a beautiful world ugly emotions are very often unwittingly generated.

For the one who is walking the way of the contemplative, who is seeking to express something of experiential wisdom, the challenge of our day is both to recognise the validity of the great aspirations which beckon society forward and at the same time cultivate the capacity to carry them forward, not on the energies of reaction but from that 'free space' where vision and aspiration are expressed in an all-powerful creativity.

Self-observation and silence

As we have already seen, human beings have the capacity to reason, to react and to respond creatively. No aspect of this tripartite creature is to be rejected. And the process of a prolonged education for this being must have as its ultimate aim the bringing into a working harmony of all these parts. For this reason we need to cultivate the capacity for self-observation. Here the word 'observation' comprehends more than a seeing for a balanced self-observation also contains the element of listening to oneself. Such a seeing and a listening immediately raises the question of 'who is observing whom?' We shall examine this question later in the learning process. For the present, establishing the meditative practice is our chief concern.

Self-observation takes place in the context of 'silence'. This we have already begun to experience in meditation.

The world in which most of us live does not easily concede the space for external silence. Failure to recognise and to respect the capacity we have for a non-sensual awareness creates not only an abhorrence but also a fear of silence. So when the 'accidental' noises of the twentieth century appear to be diminishing, it is the common custom in contemporary society to fill the silence with the sounds of speech, movement and music. Such self-protection against noiselessness is by no means confined to secular society.

A fellow priest with some trepidation announced to his flock at an occasion of corporate worship, 'We shall now have fifteen minutes' silence and learn to be still in the presence of God.' His trepidation was well justified. Following the service he was met by general negative reaction and the remark, 'What a waste of time, we could have sung quite a lot of hymns!' The crestfallen innovator muttered to himself, 'Yes, at God!'

Yet some silence, if we are determined to set about creating it, is possible for all. What is its value? External silence is of value in so far as it leads beyond itself and opens the door into interior silence. The conditions are then right for the opening of an inner ear. For far from being a vacuum, the silence to which this opening finds access contains many octaves of sound, sound which operates below the level of consciousness.

The harmonies of these octaves to which we now become attuned have nothing to do with our physical capacity for hearing. This silent music, like the high frequency of the natural world, is beyond the capacity of natural human beings to hear.

This world is also beyond the reach of those who are emotionally centred. Those who are thus bound can reach no further than sense-perception and into what is commonly called the psychic world. The still or heart centre is the one means of access.

The understanding acquired in this manner is no fanciful speculation. Its appreciation, as with all valid spiritual disciplines, is to do with everyday living. It has to do with the whole human being and with the working out of fullness of living on this planet.

All great spiritual leaders and teachers have recognised the necessity and value of silence for spiritual growth. The combination of uncontrolled thoughts and an unleashed tongue have been seen invariably as the great enemies of our potential for seeing and hearing beyond sense-perception.

The great Hindu yogis retreated into the Himalayan mountains to be alone with God, and Indian ascetics would often spend many years in the seclusion of the forest before entering upon a teaching ministry. Sometimes this very ministry would be exercised in total silence. In modern times such silent communication has been exemplified in and through Mother Meera during her frequent visits to Europe from India. Mother Meera is an Indian mystic and most of what she communicates is through silence.

The Master Jesus as a prelude to his three years of teaching spent long periods in the seclusion of the desert, and from time to time he would take the closest of his disciples up into the silence of a mountain, there to commune with his Heavenly Father. When the crucial question was put to him by the Roman Governor, 'What is truth?' he gave no verbal answer. His very presence was the authentic reply.

Contemplative religious communities from a great diversity of traditions have through the centuries built up their community life and the rhythm of their corporate worship around long periods of silence. Monks and nuns from the far reaches of Tibet to rural Sussex commit themselves to a life of listening and watching in silence. We may pose the question for what are they listening and watching?

In one such monastery in the south of England I received what for me was a dramatic and personal reply to the question. I had asked to see the Superior and was granted an interview. As the Abbess appeared behind the traditional grille my very thoughts were brought to a halt by the great aura of stillness by which she was surrounded. Intuitively I kept silent and waited. We had never met before and I assumed she knew nothing about me. How wrong I was! With a few carefully chosen words she uncovered my very thoughts and laid bare what I recognised as my deepest need. I had anticipated that this would be the opportunity for me to ask many questions. As it was I asked nothing except for her prayers. I left her presence knowing that I had been greatly blessed. I knew also that this blessing had been born in the silence of this great lady.

Departing from the monastery I pondered on the words of a Benedictine monk, Dom Bede Griffiths:

> *Inner stillness is necessary if we are to be in perfect control of our faculties, and if we are to hear the voice of the Spirit speaking to us. There can be no stillness without discipline, and the discipline of external silence can help us towards that inner tranquillity which is at the heart of authentic religious experience . . . stillness within one individual can affect society beyond measure.*

The Universal Christ (Darton, Longman and Todd, 1990)

Sacred space and sacred writings

There is a clear criterion by which this growth in understanding may be judged, for the silent harmony within, the harmony of the interior world, communicates itself immediately and inevitably to the physical world and the ability to live harmoniously with myself and others and to relate fully to the age in which I live. The intangible thus gives birth to the tangible, the hidden and secret manifests openly, and that which is intuitively known is incarnated into experiential wisdom.

A child when it is learning to walk is not required to learn from adults the theory of walking. The capacity to move its limbs so as to enable co-ordinated movement emerges from within. Given the space in which to test out a new-found ability, arms, legs, the whole torso quickly come together in an harmonious whole. Frequently there will be a goal ahead upon which the eye will be fixed, for the infant, propelled by new-found capability, wills to exercise its inherited right to walk the earth.

This is the potential of which we become increasingly aware through the practice of self-observation. The journey ahead may be well beyond my comprehension. There will be difficulties along the way, and we may frequently falter and question. Yet undergirding a new self-assurance is the knowledge that we have an 'inherited right to walk the earth' and to realise our full potential as human beings.

In the analogy of the newly walking child I referred to the space within which to test out this new-found ability. We may develop the analogy further, for the 'space' is a kind of arena, a theatre around which are those who encourage, affirm and confirm. All of us need encouragement, affirmation and confirmation, and there are well tried ways by which this is effected.

Paramount amongst these is that of 'Sacred Writings'. Under this heading I include not only the Scriptures of the world religions but the inspired writings of all those who have followed the path of experiential wisdom. And be assured by the law of like calling to like that increasingly you will come across their writings. How should they be used?

As we have already seen, the assumption that to acquire information will automatically promote growth in understanding is a fallacy. The brain is capable of storing a vast amount of factual information, and the more the memory is taxed the more its capacity will extend. It constitutes, therefore, a vast storehouse of information, but there is no inevitable connection between collecting information and experiencing it. Indeed, the accumulation of facts about God, human beings and eternal realities may powerfully militate against spiritual awakening, for the intellect was always a deceiver and is quick to say 'I know' when what it really meant is 'I am informed about'. St Augustine wrote, 'There is in the mind no knowledge of God except that it does not know Him.'

Yet Scriptures and inspired writings, if rightly used, exercise a very powerful function in relation to affirming and confirming 'the people of the way'.

It is first of all important to distinguish between the 'letter' and the 'spirit'. To follow the letter of such writings is to touch them at a superficial and analytical level. To do this is an exercise of the intellect. This is the academic approach, which of course has its place in the study of origins, etc., etc. The mystic or contemplative will seek to touch the Scriptures at the level of the 'Spirit'. What does this mean and how is it achieved?

All sacred writings channel a dynamic which operated powerfully in and through the writers and compilers. A literal approach to and interpretation of the text may well fail to touch the dynamic, for like always calls to like. Approaching the Scriptures contemplatively brings us into immediate resonance with that very dynamic which gave them birth. We see that for which we are attuned to look and we hear that which we are ready to hear.

In the community to which I belong sacred Scripture is read by the leader of the daily morning act of worship. Following the reading, which normally carries one main thought, all present are invited to share 'what they heard'. This is not an occasion either for analysis of the Scriptures or for discussion and debate, but a speaking from the heart. It is always the case that no two people have heard the same thing!

When we approach sacred writings with a listening and looking from the heart we touch their essence and spirit. There follows an explosion of understanding within the consciousness.

To search the Scriptures using the wrong faculty and without the right motivation is to misuse them, to wield them in the hand like a weapon for attacking others' beliefs and opinions is to abuse them. Their highest function is to confirm and only that can be confirmed which is already dawning within the consciousness. Khahil Gibran writes in his book *The Prophet*: 'No man can reveal to you aught but that which already lies half asleep in the dawning of your knowledge.'

The Scriptures should be approached with great reverence. Such reverence is shown by using them with economy. 'Bible Study' as such may be an interesting and informative occupation. By itself it has no direct relationship to spiritual awakening and growth. We see and hear that to which we are already attuned. It is therefore best read and heard following, not preceding, the practice of meditation.

Teachers and messengers

Let us look again at the picture of the child, struggling to exercise its new-found powers, aware of the space which is opening up ahead. Newly discovered potential and power will soon lead into new circumstances and a new power to choose for itself will be manifesting.

As a new world of choice opens up before the people of the way the question will inevitably be posed, 'How can I be sure of being guided aright, and where should I look for guidance? Who is my teacher?'

The function of any genuine teacher, whether his title be Guru, Priest, Spiritual Director or Soul Friend, is to be a signpost for the seeker, no more and no less. If the relationship is to be fruitful there must be complete trust on the part of the disciple, but no teacher has this by right. Such trust must be evoked by the sense of acceptance, freedom and security which is imparted. The chief aim of such a guide must be to lead the disciple to the finding of the Inner Teacher, i.e., the Light within. His or her role is that primarily of a catalyst and to become as quickly as possible dispensible.

This concept of the perfect teacher is delightfully portrayed in the book *Mary Poppins* by P.L. Travers. Mary Poppins with her magical powers comes suddenly into a very distraught and unbalanced family situation. As the perfect catalyst Mary Poppins first further disrupts, then brings the whole family together in a new harmony. Having completed her task she withdraws as suddenly as she came, her departure hardly noticed by those she reconciled.

It is well said that, 'When the pupil is ready the teacher will be sent', and the 'teacher' may come in a multitude of guises. They come as messengers. This is the meaning of the word 'angel'. Such angel messengers are authenticated by the fact that they never draw attention to themselves. They always point beyond. We see this dramatically portrayed in the story of the birth of Christ. The angels appear in the skies, pointed the shepherds in the right direction, then disappeared.

A preoccupation with possible or potential messengers invariably means that we miss the message. The typical nineteenth-century portrayal of angels as romantic beings borne aloft by huge wings has effectively blurred their true image. They are harbingers of 'truth', not in the sense of a package deal of beliefs, prohibitions and laws. Rather they are perfect prompters awakening us to the 'truth of a situation' within which we find ourselves. Sometimes they appear in forms of flesh and blood. They are frequently invisible.

From where do they come and from whom are they sent?

They too are part of the totality of my being. It is misleading to think of them privately in terms of space and places. Angels also reside within our consciousness and reveal themselves to the childlike, i.e., those who like children have trusting and open minds.

They prompt within the ordinary towards the extraordinary. The difficulty with most of us for much of the time is that our attention is focused in the wrong direction. We look for some kind of Divine intervention, or for 'signs from the heavens'. The heaven which is ready to open for us lies within. It is from there that angelic impulses come and it is there that we find Divine guidance, i.e., through shifts in our own consciousness. When this happens we see existing events in a different way. Ordinary people and mundane happenings assume a new significance. The natural becomes supernatural. People and the world around us do not change, but we do. As a result we see that to which we had hitherto been blind, and hear those things until now beyond our hearing.

This unveiling can only take place when we have learned a little of the art of listening and seeing. So we begin to see meaning where previously there had appeared to be none; the coincidental becomes part of a pattern. When this begins to happen the true significance of communication with God, the Divine Source, dawns upon us. We are not struggling to find and learn about God 'out there'. Rather is this God striving to break through into our consciousness.

Prayer

I have used the phrase 'listening and looking', and this activity is at the very heart not only of contemplative meditation but also of what has traditionally been called prayer. The word meditation has taken the place of prayer in the vocabulary of contemporary spirituality. Experientially the two are frequently synonymous: openness to the divine source is the characteristic of contemplative meditation and what we commonly describe as prayer. When the pivotal point of meditation is a focused openness and when that openness is to the Light which emanates from and leads to the Source, then without doubt we are also at prayer. This we shall practise in the next meditations.

Nevertheless it is true that the word prayer is, in the minds of many who are treading a spiritual path, almost an anathema because of what for them are unacceptable interpretations of the word.

The very phrase 'let us pray' as reiterated in public worship has powerful overtones for many people, suggesting the total abasement of the creature in the presence of the Creator. Equally unhelpful for those struggling to realise their God-given potential are corporate endless reiterations of human worthlessness in the presence of Divine perfection. This is not to deny nor minimise our imperfections and failings, rather is it to assert that the focussing upon unrealised potential has the power to spur the pilgrim on to ever greater achievements, whereas persistent and often masochistic metaphorical breast-beating is likely to paralyse the will and destroy all vision.

For the mystic prayer is a joyful establishing of and affirming and confirming unity with a Divine plan extending far beyond his or her personal life. This plan enfolds every individual. Wherever human beings move away from introverted self-concern and give themselves to a greater good, there prayer is being offered, regardless of what it is called, for this is the opening of the heart.

> *Prayer is not verbal. It is from the heart.*
> *To merge into the heart is prayer*
>
> SHRI RAMANA MAHARASHI

The 'establishment of unity', this 'focused openness' is the creating of a two-way channel. A devout peasant in the sixteenth century was asked what he understood by prayer. He replied, 'My Lord and I we sit and look at each other. Sometimes He speaks to me and I speak back. Always He smiles at me and that makes me smile too.'

Prayer is to enter into communion with God or the Source. At its highest peak it becomes true contemplation. Here it is wordless. It is a merging of human consciousness with the Divine. At the centre of the prayerful state is the stilling of the mind. 'Be still and know that I am God,' wrote the Jewish poet. Prayer opens up a channel between my deep centre and God, so there is intercommunion between the human and the Divine. In the opened heart is the prayer that does not cease.

In the next meditational exercises we shall develop our awareness of this creating of a two-way channel. As we have already seen, it is the Light which is the focus of our attention, Light which not only symbolises but also signifies Divinity. Our awareness of this Light is also our response to its 'ever presence', and to rest expectantly in this Light is to be at prayer.

MEDITATION EXERCISE

REFLECTION

Reflecting upon my journey so far, I embrace with thankfulness that I have the God-given capacity to hear and to see and the will to respond. And because I am already walking the way of prayer I ask for discernment that I may use those facilities and thus avoid the trap of ever learning yet never coming to a knowledge of the truth.

I remind myself that all around me are signposts towards reality and that there are messages and messengers to guide me.

In spite of doubts, shortcomings real and imagined, false starts and lack of patience with myself I press onward to see, to know and to enter into new understandings of the Way. I take comfort from the promise:

To those who gaze, a lamp am I
To those who know, a mirror
To those who knock, a door am I
To those who fare, the way

SISTER JOYCE (Omega Order)

and to this I respond 'Amen'.

IMAGINATION

With the eye of the imagination I look again at the Way ahead.
The road has broadened and now I perceive both on my left
hand and on my right fellow-travellers. Here and there by the
roadside are small groups, textbooks in hand, engaged in
earnest debate about the nature of the signs which point
onward. Their wording and language is providing meaty material for detailed discussion.

I turn my attention to those who are walking by my side.
There is a clear sense of purpose about them all, yet no hurry.
All have time to reach out hands of friendship, and from them I
derive comfort and encouragement to keep walking in the
Light.

INTUITION

From reflection and imagination we move again step by step
through the process of relaxation and awareness of the Light. I
am aware again of being linked at the level of the heart in a vast
network of light joining all the people of the way and encom-
passing the globe. I rest in the stillness.

I close and confirm my meditation with the words:

'Tis only the splendour of Light hideth Thee.

7

The Mystic and Healing

I am sure that there are many energies in the Universe as yet untapped which God means us to use to make wounded spirits whole. I want to help release them without descending to magic or superstition.

LESLIE WEATHERHEAD, *Wounded Spirits*
(Hodder, 1962)

Following my ordination as a priest I was given responsibility for a large new housing estate. 'Responsibility', it seemed to me at the time, chiefly consisted of persuading the inhabitants that the large architecturally anonymous building which had recently appeared on the edge of the estate was a desirable place for them to meet on Sundays. Few over a period of years were thus persuaded. Nevertheless, relationships of friendship and trust were established and these led to invitations to share in many family crises.

I was brought into one such crisis late one night by a frantic banging on my front door. A young couple in great distress pleaded, 'Will you come with us at once to the hospital, our baby is dying.' Their three-month-old daughter, suffering from an obscure disease, according to the doctor had only hours to live.

As we sat around the bed in the intensive care unit I was acutely aware of having become the focal point of the parents' hope and expectancy. I had known the family for some time.

They were not religious. Indeed they had once labelled them-selves as 'unbelievers in anything'. Yet now they were clearly looking for 'something' and associating it with me. Intuitively I laid my hands on the baby's head, and opened myself to 'all that constituted the greater good for that child and its parents'. At that moment I was aware within myself of both agnosticism and faith. There were many questions which I could not answer, yet I knew that in the face of the God in whom I trusted was compassion for the child and its parents.

I saw consternation in the face of the nurse and for a moment thought that the child had gone. Then with a look of clear unbelief she assured me that 'temperature and pulse were normal'. The child was going to live.

From that moment I have never doubted that the spiritual path has to do with healing. To place myself in the context of Light as we have been learning to do on our journey is to become part of a healing dynamic. And here it is important that we are clear as to what we mean by healing. The phrase I have used to describe the healing of the dying baby is that of the effecting of a 'greater good'. As finite beings, whatever our knowledge – be it scientific, theological or medical – we know only in part. We cannot with certainty know what constitutes the greater good of any human being. Physical healing may or may not contribute to the experiencing of this greater good. When healing is viewed from this perspective it assumes much greater dimensions than that of physical restoration.

A colleague of mine concerned to exercise a 'ministry of healing', visited a sick 'believer' in hospital. At the very moment when hands were laid upon him he died! I have no doubt that leaving the physical body in this manner may be part of a healing process, for the physical dimension is but one aspect of our full humanity.

What part has touch or the use of the hands to play at this level of healing? To this question I would reply 'No primary part.' It has value and significance only as a focal point for the healing dynamic.

I have reflected many times on the healing of the dying child. What exactly were the positive factors within the situation? To speak of 'Divine Intervention' begs too many questions, not least about the nature of such a God. Yet clearly there was a kind of intervention. The natural course of events was halted, a supernormal power entered into the situation and effected physical healing. I am sure that the experiencing of this supernormal power had to do with a conscious commitment by a number of involved compassionate people to the 'greater good'.

At the time of the hospital visit a network of friends who were all committed to what they expressed as 'holding sick people in the Light' were doing just that. Simple people, most would have found great difficulty in answering the problem of why some of those whom they held in the Light recovered and others died. Sophisticated explanations were quite beyond them. They themselves had learned to walk in the Light and, though agnostic about explanations, they knew experientially that the Light expressed the compassionate face of God. They walked the way of experiential wisdom.

It is important to note the phrase used by the compassionate group, 'holding in the Light'. To hold implies the recognition of a space within which 'the greater good' can work its will. To seek to impose my will upon the situation is to assume that my knowledge is perfect and that what I know is best. This may quickly become an egotistic attempt to control. To do this is to cease being a channel for the greater good.

A channel for divine power

Let us look a little closer at what we may understand by this supernatural power, power which we have so far defined simply as the Light. Before attempting a definition we remind ourselves again that articulations and explanations are not to be identified with the reality itself. As we have seen, experiential wisdom, the mystical consciousness, cannot be equated with nor be claimed as the prerogative of any one pattern of beliefs.

From the time of the healing of the apparently dying child I found myself facing a challenge to my very conception of God. Five years had been spent studying His shape and nature through the medium of theology, philosophy and psychology, all supported by an intensive study of the Holy Scriptures. It seemed that I was well equipped to understand everything but God.

Again and again there echoed in my mind a phrase from the Scriptures: 'I now realise how true it is that God does not have favourites but accepts people from everywhere.' (The Acts of the Apostles, 10). This, I thought, was no proper basis for a powerful and authoritarian preaching ministry, yet it clearly fitted in with what was happening in my life. My experience of what, to my horror, people were beginning to refer to as my 'healing ministry' was pointed clearly in the direction of a God who appeared quite indifferent to religious labels or creeds. If anything, He appeared to favour those who lived out their lives hovering between atheism and agnosticism.

When asked by a curious 'outsider' what kind of people gathered in my church, I found myself replying that I supposed at least ninety percent were benevolent agnostics: benevolent otherwise they would not be there, agnostic because credal statements were for most of them little more than mumbo jumbo, to be put up with as a price for what just might prove to be an interesting talk after all that had been disposed of.

I found myself asking the question: 'Who is this God for whom I wear my collar back to front?' Clearly He was getting larger and larger and it was becoming more and more difficult to fit Him into His own institution.

In Chapter 1, I referred to my dramatic exist from a stifling kind of religious box. This exit involved for me a reinterpretation of the tradition in which I had been both nurtured and smothered. With the awakening of a new faculty for hearing, words which had become shibboleths and jargon took upon themselves a larger and fresh significance. I saw that what Christians call the Christ is the Divine principle active in and through the whole created order, and that this 'Christ' principle may be defined as energy – not an impersonal energy, but the highest of all energies, that of love. I saw also that this energy is seeking to manifest itself at all levels of Creation, through a process of evolution. Through this evolutionary action the Universal Christ is struggling to come to birth. The process is one of struggle for it is taking place in a universe where manifestly there is disharmony, disintegration and conflict. The struggle is towards and for the harmonising of the universe, that is universal harmony. The end of this evolutionary process will be the perfect manifestation of this Divine principle in and through the cosmos; the harmonising of all things; the true meaning of Christ's 'Second Coming'.

The spearhead of this struggle is manifested within the human kingdom. It is a struggle between human egocentricity and divisiveness on the one hand and the Divine principle which creates wholeness on the other. Whenever, in the history of humanity, individuals or groups have aligned themselves with this evolutionary struggle, facets of true humanity have broken through and healing and wholeness is effected. It is within this context of meaning and purpose for humanity that those who are following the contemplative path find themselves to be channels of healing.

Where do these channels lead and how does such healing operate? So far we have observed this happening in the healing of an individual and in physical restoration. This is part of the picture, for the mystic relates not only to individual human beings but in a corporate sense to the beingness of humans. For this reason, far from constituting an isolated pietism, mysticism has from first to last a social significance. This is brought into being through the realisation by every mystic of being part of the 'universal or cosmic being'. This awareness stems from what we have described as alignment with the universal energy of love.

Mysticism and healing

Is there a distinctly mystical approach to healing and wholeness? I believe there is.

The first and most distinctive characteristic is that of an egoless linking to the universal energy. It is egoless because it is not
the exercise of the human will, an attempt to persuade God to
act in a particular manner or to intervene in what otherwise
would appear to be a hopeless situation. It is an aligning of the
human will with that of the Creator.

From this it will be seen that a healing activity or ministry is
not something added on to the life or an adjunct to other pre-
occupations. It is to be seen as central to the energy which
flows out from the whole life, a communicating wholeness.

Jesus of Nazareth, whose three years prior to his death were
characterised by works of healing, replied in answer to his crit-
ics, 'I must do the work of my Father,' and 'My Father is
working so also must I'. All this healing activity sprang from a
conscious union with the Source.

Such a union, far from being a static fatalism, is also a linking
to the ongoing Divine activity, a recognition that the Creation
is not a once-for-all single act somewhere in the distant past but
part of an unceasing process.

As our consciousness becomes centred in the reality of what
has been called this 'eternal regeneration', so do we learn to
perceive the direction which it is taking, and as co-workers
together with God we give place, space and full recognition to
this redemptive activity.

When this happens the apparently impossible becomes possible. At the heart of mystical healing is, as we saw in the case of
the Abbess, the catalytic effect of a life which is focussed in the
direction of a greater or cosmic good. The direction of a life
may be changed. Rigid minds are broken down, positive attitudes are brought to birth in negative situations, and antago-
nisms give way to goodwill. This is to hold people and
circumstances in the Light. It is healing indeed, and to this the

mystic is called. It is to put into effect the great prayer of Francis of Assisi:

> *Lord make me an instrument of your peace,*
> *Where there is hatred let me sow love;*
> *Where there is injury, pardon;*
> *Where there is doubt, faith,*
> *Where there is despair, hope;*
> *Where there is darkness, light . . .*

During the Second World War the English city of Coventry, during one terrible night, was devastated by wave after wave of enemy bombers. For miles around the sky was lit up by a blazing inferno. The city was engulfed in flames and great numbers of people died.

The following morning those who had survived the holocaust emerged from their shelters to find that medieval Coventry had gone for ever, but in the midst of the destruction the spire of the fifteenth-century cathedral remained. The body of the church was in ruins. Some of the walls remained standing. A magnificent building had become an empty shell.

What remained of the high altar was covered with rubble and charred beams. As dawn broke and before the work of clearing away the fallen masonry had begun the Provost cleared a way to the altar through the rubble, and picking up two charred beams bound them together to form a cross. This he placed above the altar with the words, 'Father Forgive . . .'. During the fifty years that have followed those charred beams have remained as a symbol of reconciliation and healing. As a terrible retribution for the destruction of the city, Dresden in Germany was bombed with even greater ferocity, killing even greater numbers. Yet after the war had ended these two cities were the very first to come together with mutual forgiveness. Groups of young people from each city travelled to rebuild what their respective nations had destroyed. A great ministry of reconciliation had begun.

Millions now know the story of Coventry and Dresden. Very few know that through the years week by week without fail a group of very ordinary people have met weekly in the crypt beneath the Coventry ruins. Known simply as the 'Healing Group' and attracting no attention they have exercised a ministry of healing which has without doubt influenced multitudes.

A nation's safety, it has been said, depends upon the number of its contemplatives. However we interpret this – and we shall examine this later – it is certainly true that it is through the contemplative awareness of those who are following the way of the heart that an evolution of human consciousness is maintained and developed and ideals allied to capacity. Their corporate intention forms the spearhead of the movement against human egocentricity and at the same time draws humanity away from self-centredness into the Light and into the process of transformation.

The ancient symbol of this is that of the cross. The vertical line signifies the union of the earthly kingdoms with the heavenly, whilst the horizontal reaches out towards and draws into this union all humanity.

I have used the phrase 'all humanity', but this requires qualification, for whilst the healing energies are ever seeking to enfold and to permeate human need at every level, all humans contain elements of free will and the energies of love can never violate that freedom to choose. I quote again from the *Omega Vision*:

> *Within the shapes and shadows we call human*
> *Are mirrored all those parts*
> *Which science and the senses have divided.*
> *The essences of all creation there exist*
> *Each giving to the other, yet not all*
> *For that is mirrored only, which to the mirror*
> *Shows its face . . . .*

Because we consciously turn our faces towards the Light and because we allow the Light to lead us onward, a magnetic attraction is put into operation, and as a result there are those who 'show their faces to the mirror'. This drawing power is quite apart from and other than the persuasive power of speech or the emotional fervour generated by the evangelist. The former is the law of like calling to like, and evoking spontaneous response. The latter is the application of external pressure.

At a very critical point in my own life I felt this drawing power to the extent that the direction of my life was changed. It happened in and through the most mundane of circumstances. At the end, as it seemed at the time, of my spiritual tether I found myself invited to spend a weekend with one whose life was characterised by holiness, i.e., wholeness. The catalytic effect on my life was brought about not by exhortation nor advice and certainly not by admonition, but by his appearance in my bedroom with the dawn, bearing a cup of tea. And with this act came healing of the mind.

Intersection

The ground of all true healing is generated by and flows from the quiet mind as affirmed in the words of the Jewish poet: 'Thou O God will keep him in perfect peace whose mind is stayed on Thee.'

The healing ministry manifests at many levels. An important aspect is brought into operation through the mystic's integration into contemporary society, for to follow this path is to know that we are in a real sense children of the age in which we live. It is here that we find ourselves living within a paradox, i.e., standing at a point of intersection between the unseen and the seen, the hidden life which is the source of our motivation and inspiration and involvement with the real needs of that society of which we are an integral part. It is this operating at points of intersection which is at the heart of healing.

Intersection may be described as standing at a point between two worlds which at the level of rational thought are in contradiction, but which at a deeper level are seen to be one.

We have already looked at this as it operated historically in the experience of the mystics. Emerging from the heart of all great religions, they find themselves within conflicting belief patterns which superficially divide them. In their common experience of the Divine love and their touching of reality they are united. Of intersection F.C. Happold writes as follows:

It would be misleading to think of intersection as a purely intelligent process . . . rather a union of spiritual intuition and rational thought is brought into play . . . and the intellect ceases to be the only instrument of knowing.

Religious Faith in Twentieth Century Man
(Darton, Longman and Todd, 1980)

I recall within my own experience a dramatic example of discovering a religious community living powerfully at an unusual point of intersection. I had been invited to visit a convent 'to teach some contemplative dance'. Assuming that the community would be very 'modern' in every sense I was very surprised to meet with all the trappings of medieval monasticism – grilles, veils, traditional habits and apparent seclusion from the world.

These were outward and visible forms, but I quickly discovered that operating behind this traditional exterior was a very powerful dynamic of freedom and joy reaching out to the needs of a world which was not 'outside' but in the hearts of the nuns. Standing within an ancient tradition and maintaining both its respect and respect for it, they operated at the heart of contemporary society.

Simone Weil, a Jewish mystic who died shortly after the Second World War, was a remarkable example of living at points of intersection. Remaining faithful to her Jewish origins, she nevertheless had an intense realisation of the essence of the

Christian faith, but without any kind of exclusiveness. Everything became for her what she described as 'Christified'. 'I came to feel,' she writes, 'that Plato was a mystic, that all the *Iliad* was bathed in a Christian Light and that the *Bhagavad Gita* was as creative as the New Testament.'

This capacity to stand at points of intersection applies not only in the world of religion and specifically spiritual issues but in all areas of life. We may see this, for example, in the world of politics. Two opposed and opposing parties will at the level of concepts and policy statements represent two apparently irreconcilable policies and groupings. The mystic will see that the real divisions are not those between the two parties, but that at the level of motivation and disinterested public service the real divisions may well operate within the two parties, not between them.

The healing ministry in such a situation is to recognise the positive elements on both sides of the divide and in recognising them to give them space for growth. From this it will be seen that standing at such a point of intersection we are also involved in a ministry of reconciliation. I quote again from F.C. Happold:

> *As I draw to the end of a long and active life I have come to regard a capacity for intersection as perhaps the most essential quality of mind and spirit needed by twentieth century man.'*

Happold saw intersection and its application to all areas of life as significant for the uncovering of the dynamic of evolution in our time. As we move into the twenty-first century it is intersection which will increasingly open doors within society, moving from the unreal to the touching of the real.

Time and eternity

It is this capacity to distinguish between the real and the unreal that will become the hallmark of evolving human beings in the twenty-first century. This is the dynamic which the people of the way have responsibility for nurturing. There is no division or separation between this and the fostering of my own growth and progress. To minister to my own real needs is to minister to the needs of others.

Times set aside for meditation are periods for the conscious cultivation of impulses at all times present: the practice of a presence that is all-pervading, opening to a dynamic which is leading ever forward, bringing healing in its wake.

To pursue such a path requires that we stand at all times at a point of intersection between time and eternity. From perspectives taken from outside of time, i.e., from the 'Still Centre' we begin to understand the meaning of time. We become conscious links between time and eternity. In his *Four Quarters* T.S. Eliot describes this as the still point of the turning world where past and future are gathered. Here we may stand beyond time and its limitations in order to learn its true significance. This is the threshold, this the point of intersection where we must learn to stand if we are to understand and transmit all that pertains to healing and wholeness in our day. It is the only source of valid vision.

In the Jewish Scriptures frequent use is made of the imagery of the Watchman. The function of the Watchman was to patrol the walls of the enclosed city. He was in effect its eyes and its ears. From the ramparts he held a commanding view of all that was taking place. He alone in the city could command a picture of the whole. From sunset until dawn the cry would echo periodically from within the confines of the city: 'Watchman, what of the night?'

We noted earlier the saying that 'A nation's safety depends on the number of its contemplatives'. They are the watchmen in any society. They alone occupy a vantage point between and above separated communal interests. The plan and purpose to which they are committed transcends all divisions. It can never be encapsulated within exclusive groupings, whether religious, political or social. The contemplative is acutely aware of these divisions and at the same time perceives the superficial nature of the walls and boundaries which at the level of thoughts and ideologies perpetuate such groupings.

As the 'people of the way' we are also pilgrims. The word implies movement, movement prompted from 'the still point of the turning world'. So we move easily across all barriers.

This is the freedom which authenticates the journey of uncovery and discovery which we are following. So do we stand as reconcilers and healers at points of intersection in a divided world.

MEDITATION EXERCISE

REFLECTION

We claim no special knowledge other than that which is knowable to the human heart. We live and move and have our being at points of tension between many paradoxes. Respecting all forms we are dependent on none. If necessity so requires, we are prepared to live and operate within conventional and traditional situations for the sake of the 'greater good'. Seeking always to be centred in the heart, we touch that source by which the intellect is activated. Seeing clearly into the world of spirit, we are grounded by our disciplines into the world of matter. Committed to a vision which goes far beyond individual spirituality, we recognise the infinite worth of each person. Looking into the future, we strive always to live in the present moment.

So do we become one with that universal energy, that evolutionary force which is ever striving to manifest within human consciousness.

IMAGINATION

Using my imagination I see again the straight path and bring into the picture my companions, fellow people of the way, and as I look I perceive clearly the great variety of human beings represented.

I see also that converging on to the straight path and on either side are many minor roads along which pilgrims are travelling. Towards all of them from wherever they come I feel a warmth and as we meet I welcome them. I am aware that I need their company. They will tell me of events and experiences which drew them towards the straight path, and this will strengthen me on the journey. I look ahead to the point towards which all are converging, and see the sun rising above the distant horizon. Gradually every pathway and traveller is bathed in light and I remember the words of a watchman far back in history: 'Unto you who honour my name the sun of righteousness shall rise with healing in its wings' (Malachi 4)

INTUITION

Passing from imagination to contemplation, I give myself, as before, the time and space to relax and to become body-conscious. I acknowledge my body to be both a receptacle and a channel of healing.

I centre in the heart and from there with my outbreathing surround the known and the unknown with the healing light.

I affirm and confirm my meditation with the words:

You are the light of the world; a city that is set on a hill cannot be hid.

Matthew 5

8

Relationships and the Human Condition

I consider that our present sufferings are not worth compar-
ing with the glory that will be revealed in us. The creation
waits in eager expectation for the children of God to be
revealed . . . We wait eagerly for our adoption as children,
the redemption of our bodies.

ST. PAUL, Romans 8

It is impossible to follow the straight path of the mystic without before long coming face to face with the problem of human relationships. All of us know that most of life's difficulties can be identified as people – other people! For without other people and the difficulties they create, the business of living would be pleasanter and much easier. In a word other people are the difficulty and the mystic is no exception!

But the difficulty cannot be quite so simply defined, and this is for two reasons: the first is that we are all other people to someone else, and the second is that all of us in some way require other people. At the highest level we need them for growth into maturity and at the lowest as props on which to lean. Those who try to dispense with other people frequently resort consciously or unconsciously to substituting inanimate objects or animals for human beings. So how are we to face the problem?

We must first of all stand back and look at the human condition as a whole before tackling the problem of personal relationships. And to bring this right into the context of experiential wisdom we shall do so by evolving further our meditational exercises involving intellect, imagination and intuition. To effect this we shall observe ourselves entering into a series of pictures which portray both the tragedy and triumph of the human condition.

Having decided consciously to follow this meditative exercise you use your imagination and permit yourselves to move along the path into an area where there is great darkness. This darkness is that of a great shadow falling across the path.

The human shadow

At first we are unable to grasp either the size or the shape of the shadow. We are conscious only of the intensity of the darkness. This is the shadow cast by the great Prison House of Humanity. We are face to face with the human predicament, the nature of the human being.

We are now touching within ourselves the psyche of all humanity (for we are not apart and separate from this picture). We are awakening to the truth that humanity by the fact of its constitution and conditioning is caught up with all creation upon the great wheel of eternal recurrence. The human being is of the earth, earthy. From this we have taken form and to this by its gravitational pull we must inevitably return. The whole creation is involved in this perpetual cycle of birth, death and re-creation. It is within this inexorable law that both the suffering and the hope exist.

We look again at the shadow and in our imagination we see on its periphery a large and man-made structure. This is in the nature of a scaffolding. Upon this scaffolding we see a great many people. Each one is engaged in intense concentrated activity. Yet each activity takes place within a separated and confined space. All are seated and none move from their own place and space.

The activities with which these workers are so preoccupied cover a wide range of skills. There on the scaffolding are writers, artists and craftsmen of many kinds applying themselves to the work of taking the measurements of the shadow. Few amongst them have any awareness of their companions, for each is dedicated exclusively to the skills of their own craft.

The overwhelming involvement of each individual is with that portion of the shadow best seen from the position they occupy upon the scaffolding and most suited to their particular capabilities. One thing they have in common. None, however skilled in their particular field, are able, from the scaffolding, properly to comprehend the shadow's shape or substance. The totality of the human condition and of its full potential eludes them.

Who are these people? They are those worthy of our respect who, though limited and partial in their perceptions, nevertheless acknowledge the existence of the shadow. They are skilled representatives of science, philosophy, psychology and religion who, since the dawning of human self-consciousness, have wrestled each in their own way with the problem which now confronts us. Yet their terms of reference are other than those by which we are travelling. Their perspective is from beyond and apart from the shadow. The way of experiential wisdom requires that we not only face the reality of the shadow's existence but that we enter into the darkness itself.

Darkness and light

Here again we find ourselves within a paradox. For as we enter into the shadow we are conscious of that Light within ourselves; an inner assurance gained from the experience of our pilgrimage so far that it is through facing and penetrating the darkness of the human condition that we shall experience an even greater light.

As we enter the darkness its true nature begins immediately

to unfold. Entrance in a state of trusting unknowing leads at once to the dawning of understanding.

The composition of the darkness is beyond our capacity to measure, but with the eyes of the heart we are able to see. The outlines of the shadow, though inconstant and vibrating with movement, have a basic shape. We look steadfastly and without fear, and with such looking comes the understanding that within this human being all humanity exists. Here all human beings are gathered into one. Here all its parts are focused.

We see that the composition of the darkness is of many parts and particles. In its essential nature it is one and uniform. The destiny of all humanity is woven into its fabric. The substance holds the elements of suffering and death. With all its parts we resonate. From the shadow there is no detachment. We are part of each other.

We move forward unafraid, for the darkness has no power to overwhelm us nor to eclipse our vision. The reason for this will become apparent when our passage through the shadow is completed. This is the true walk of faith and trust, and we hold within us the words of the great fourteenth-century mystic, Mother Julian of Norwich: 'All shall be well, and all shall be well, and all manner of things shall be well.'

As we penetrate further into the shadow our perceptions are sharpened and vision enlarged. We become aware that the very act of trust required for entering in has also effected entrance for the Light. We are not walking in darkness but are surrounded by the Light, and by its illumination the interior of the shadow becomes visible.

At this point the magnitude of the shadow becomes visible to our gaze. Its shape and its size become clear. We are standing within a vast model of a human being. We also become aware of another group of people. Unlike those on the exterior of the shadow these are constantly moving around, examining the contours of the interior. In their hands they have instruments by which they are engaged in taking measurements. They record results of these in the form of blueprints, which are then bound together to provide maps for the people of the way. These are the architects of the hidden sciences whose origins are chiefly in the East. Their access to the shadow was by another and secret way. Because of this they work only with reflected light and do not benefit experientially by the Light which shines upon the straight path. For this reason they frequently fail to perceive that the contours of the shadow are ever changing and therefore beyond the scope of those instruments by which they measure.

In the face of this ceaseless activity we need again to stand back and to centre again in that space where the Light dwells. In so doing we maintain our equilibrium and whilst recognising the skills of those by whom we are surrounded, we will know of a certainty that only in the following of the straight path can we maintain our vision.

> *And not to each shall all the picture in its every part be clear*
> *But each shall find their part within its forming*
> *The shaping of a pattern shall we see, of which we are a part*
> *Yet are we now not central to its parts or shape*
> *Though to its wholeness is our giving central*

> *The Omega Vision*

In renewing our perspectives we now observe another aspect of the shadow. We see the primary source from which it takes its substance and by which it is perpetuated. The origin of this is a ceaseless flow of energy: uncontrolled and uncontrollable emotions.

These constitute the forces by which the great mass of humanity operates. They are now the manifestation within the human being of the laws of repelling and attracting. Human likes and dislikes, attachments and aversions are seen to operate quite independently of will and intention. They are entirely reactional. These are largely ungoverned and ungovernable aspects of human nature. In unbroken stream they both pour into and issue forth from the substance of the shadow.

All this activity is instinctual, an automatic functioning of that part of the human being we hold in common with the animal kingdom. In part its manifestation is regulated by legal sanctions, ethical structures and religious ideals imposed by society upon itself for self-preservation, stability and advancement. The effects of this are what we commonly call civilisation. By this means much of the energy thus created is channelled and directed. The residue forms the substance of universal wars.

All this we see, and all this we know to be something not apart from us. Yet we are able to stand apart. We have learnt a little of how to observe with a measure of detachment, and because of this we are able to pass through the darkness to the other side of the shadow.

All-pervading light

Here we find ourselves emerging into a place of great Light. Its radiance is like that of the sun. Yet it emanates from the very substance of the shadow itself.

Viewed from where in imagination we are now standing, every particle of darkness which constitutes the shadow is seen to contain within itself a seed of brilliant light by which a process of transformation is taking place. The Being of Darkness is being changed. Its shape is assuming constancy of form and unity in all its parts. A great Being of Light is emerging from the shadow. It is in the light of the human condition as we have observed and experienced it through this meditative journey into the interior world that we can work through with knowledge the 'problem' of relationships in everyday living.

Relationship and community

Resulting from the idealism of the 1960s and the desire to create models of harmonious and loving relationships was a widespread movement to establish communities. Seen in the light of the need to achieve balance between idealism and the realistic appraisal of the human being, the success rate has not been high. The average length of life of most of the new communities is not much more than two years.

Where communities have quickly disintegrated it is almost invariably the case that there has been a lack of the great cohesive fact of commitment to a common goal. The 'why' of the community, its *raison d'être*, has been submerged beneath subjective and perpetual preoccupation with the working-out of relationships.

Where there is an understanding that not all interpersonal relationships can be sorted out at once and that some may never find complete resolution, and where the community has learned to look beyond its own 'navel', there much can be accomplished.

It has often been asserted by the idealists that the Age of Aquarius is not compatible with either structure or disciplined activity. Experience has demonstrated that when frameworks for growth are dispensed with, groups fall apart. All objectivity disappears. A member of a healthy and thriving community was heard to say, 'Come hell or high water, feel like it or not, we meet at the alloted times in the chapel'. Nothing is more likely to act as a powerful stabilising factor in community living than regular periods when people are not preoccupied with themselves. So is the community vision renewed and models of realistic and mature relationship achieved.

In the community of which I am part we practise in group situations the discipline of learning to speak from, and to listen to one another speaking from, 'the heart'. This is a conscious taking up of what we have seen to be 'uncontrolled and uncontrollable energies' from the level of instinctive and automatic reaction.

It is important to those taking part to be clear that this is not a therapy group or an occasion for unravelling the psyche. Neither is it the practice of group dynamics in the commonly understood meaning of the phrase. The name I have given to this sharing is that of 'dynamics of the free space'.

Part of the learning process which quickly develops as the group grows together is that of self-observation. Standing apart from ourselves in this way we become quickly aware of the level from which we are speaking to others. The content of such speaking is egoless, i.e., there is no desire to impress, defend or to win the support of others.

To the extent that I learn to listen to and observe myself, to that extent do I develop the capacity to hear others. A threefold operation on the part of those taking part may be described as that of head, heart and solar plexus; the head approach being that of intellectual involvement, the heart that of the 'free space' and the solar plexus that of reaction.

Whilst learning to relate in this way a group situation can powerfully promote growth in the practice of non-reactionary relationships. It is equally possible to develop this in our ordinary daily one-to-one contacts. The regular practice of centring in the heart during meditational exercise equips and prepares us to do precisely this in everyday life. To do this is surely what Jesus Christ meant when he urged his listeners to 'turn the other cheek'.

To learn to do this with what we have proved to be difficult relationships is also a significant step in the direction of seeing others in a totally new way. For it is here that I learn to look into another person without judgement or intrusion and to see beyond the exterior to which I habitually react.

Image and reality

Seeing 'beyond the exterior' requires that we are able to recognise in others the real human being hidden beyond the 'personality'. The very word 'persona' means mask, and all of us in varying degrees wear it. This mask begins to take shape very early in life; it is synonymous with the small child's discovery of the need to hide from others its real feelings, to protect itself from the world of adults and later on to project itself acceptably in social situations.

In primitive 'uncivilised' cultures the development of a persona is frequently unnecessary. The requirements of social convention do not dictate such play-acting and there is no need to project an image for the control of people and situations. The cultivation of the mask is very central to the Western world with its competitive culture. This has been developed to a very high point with the advent of the portrayal of human beings on film and television. The all-pervading pressure is to project the right, i.e., acceptable image. Increasingly the personality becomes the creation of those whose financial interests lie in its successful manipulation.

The same applies to politicians. Elections are won or lost according to the public perception of personality. Increasingly the gap between reality and the acceptable mask widens. Occasionally the mask fails through a moral lapse or the flagrant breaching of conventional behaviour. Disillusionment and cynicism result.

The substance of the personality mask is held together by the human ego which draws to itself the primitive instinct for self-preservation, assertion and competitiveness. Where these predominate to a marked degree their characteristics are clearly visible in the contours of the mask and deception becomes more difficult.

Frederick Franck in his book *The Zen of Seeing* (Wildwood House, 1973) describes some of the well known characters whose portraits he had sketched. Amongst these the most outstanding was that of Pope John XXIII who, as mentioned earlier, made a tremendous impact on the contempory world by throwing open the doors of the Roman Catholic Church in the 1960s. According to Franck, Pope John's face was the most egoless he had ever seen. His face was that of a child before donning the mask.

Personalities are cultivated in order to charm, attract and frequently to deceive. Few are impervious to such powerful influences. All the levels of society are affected and moulded by it. Frequently the most intellectually able are quite unable to see through the mask.

I recall a young man in his teens, very religious, whose influence in a particular group was extremely powerful. The power emanated from a very carefully constructed persona. In his presence few could resist his charm. John was generally regarded as a 'very spiritually mature' young man. In fact he was a ruthless manipulator. It has to be said, however, that he was almost totally unaware of his duplicity. He had learnt to play a role and to wear an appropriate mask in order to win acclaim. The sad fact was that the community to which he belonged and within which he exercised such powerful influence was a group quite unable to see through the mask or to recognise his play-acting.

In this young man's presence few could resist the pressure of his personality. The day came when he was to leave the community. A crowd gathered at the railway station to say farewell. It was as they left the station that John's friends and followers began to realise that which is frequently true when a powerful personality is withdrawn, namely that there was nothing left. A pressure was removed and before long the group became aware that John's only legacy was that of a dependence complex on the part of many within the community.

The cult of personality is as much in evidence within spiritual groups and communities as in secular society. Note the literature disseminated to advertise lecturers, facilitators and spiritual leaders of every kind. The correct persona is the all-important point of attraction and appeal, invariably presented with a broad smiling face. This reaches a point of incongruity when the subject of the presentation is a teacher from the East whose validity and integrity are attested by the undoubted spirituality which he or she represents, rather than that of an all-powerful persona.

Detachment and freedom

I have referred to looking into others without intrusion or judgement. This can be done only when we step back from the personality in question. If I am really to see another individual as they are behind the mask, then I must first of all metaphorically leave them, like John, at the railway station. I must move out of the area of magnetic attraction and see with true contemplative detachment.

It is a trite saying that 'love is blind'. Nevertheless it is true that a certain kind of loving, i.e., that of total involvement with another's emotions, makes it impossible for us to see things as they really are. We cannot objectively see other people unless there is emotional space between us. Again we find ourselves operating within a paradox, for it is as we stand back in this manner that we come close in a real sense.

There is a circle dance sometimes used as a form of greeting in the Omega Community when a group comes together for a retreat. First of all there is a step forward symbolising 'I step forward to greet you'. The second step is backwards: 'I step backward to give you space.' The third step is to the side: 'I step to the side to allow you to pursue your own way.' These three steps together symbolise the essential ingredients of interaction which takes us beyond the level of personality.

In recent years a great loosening up has entered into human relationships. We cannot deal here with many of the wide implications of this. Sufficient to say that on the whole this has represented a very healthy development. It is all part of the holistic understanding that every part of the human being is to be recognised and that the body in particular is to be taken into reverence and recognition.

What I have called loosening up is of great importance. Bodily freedom is often an important aspect of what we saw earlier as movement from the conventional stage. It is of equal importance to recognise that loosening belongs to the stage of transition. If we remain there we become both shapeless and prone to many disturbing and sometimes destructive influences. For it is at this very stage of development that we are particularly prone to the influence of personalities. Emotionally centred ourselves, we are vulnerable to the emotions of others, and our body language will quickly communicate this fact.

Such body language may be clearly demonstated by two types of physical contact when used in greeting. To clasp another person with a body hug involving the whole body belongs to the transition or 'charismatic stage'. It expresses emotions which may be excellent in themselves but nevertheless are without a clear and conscious focus. The contemplative greeting involves heart to heart physical contact. It is heartfelt recognition of one another with no kind of intrusion or invasion.

Another example of meeting and mutual recognition beyond that of personality interaction may be seen in the circle dance to which we have referred. As the participants move around they are invited to greet one another with eye contact, not the kind which has been described as 'a soulful friendship for life' look, but rather the contact that has no element of intrusion, yet which expresses and indeed conveys a love which gives complete freedom.

Agape – unconditional love

'Love' is one of the most difficult words in the English language. It has been, as we all know, debased, abused and is frequently misused. I once saw a fairly stereotyped romantic Hollywood movie. The film opened with a love scene set in New York City. The man: 'Darling I love you.' The woman: 'All over New York tonight men are saying to women "Darling, I love you" which being interpreted means "Darling I want you"'!

So far on our journey we have said little of love. Rather has love in its highest form been implied consistently by the relationship of each one of us to our divine source. How are we to understand this love and what is its place in human relationships?

As we have seen, the word is inadequate to express the wide range of meanings associated with the word. In its highest form it finds expression in the Greek *agape*. This is what we are to understand as Divine love. It involves unconditional giving, and it is to this kind of love that we have been opening ourselves in following the way of the mystic.

To open ourselves even in small measure to the reality of this love brings us into vital contact with what we have described as 'the highest energy of all', the energy of a love that is both universal and personal.

In *The Phenomenon of Man* (p. 295) Teilhard de Chardin describes the motivating power of this love:

> *We have only to note the result it produces unceasingly all around us. Is it not a positive fact that thousands of mystics have drawn from its flame a passionate fervour that outstrips by far in brightness and purity the urge and devotion of any human love? Is it not also a fact that having once experienced it, further thousands of men and women are daily renouncing every other ambition and every other joy save that of abandoning themselves to it.*

Outstanding and universally recognised witnesses to this incarnated love may be seen in the lives of such diverse characters as Mahatma Gandhi and Mother Teresa of Calcutta. They were born and bred in entirely different spiritual traditions, yet the path each followed was that of unreserved response to all the pervading love of God. Gandhi expressed it in his dedication to bringing hope to the outcasts. Mother Teresa by the same power gave herself unreservedly to the sick and dying first of all in Calcutta then, through her co-workers, to thousands beyond.

For both these spiritual giants the great ikon of the love which emanated from their lives was that of Jesus on the Cross.

This was expressed for Gandhi in the words of his favourite hymn:

> *When I survey the wondrous Cross,*
> *On which the Prince of Glory died*
> *My richest gain I count but loss*
> *And pour contempt on all my pride.*

Can we, indeed should we, be learning to offer this love to all? The answer to this must be an unequivocal yes. At the same time we need to recognise the clear difference between liking and loving. We can indeed, as far as we are able, offer *agape* by giving space, place and recognition of their needs and rights to others. We cannot possibly like everybody.

Liking and disliking, attraction and repulsion between individuals is commonly spoken of as to do with 'chemistry' between people. More accurately we may call it mutual responses and reactions at the personality level. Liking or disliking has no moral content. What we do about this does.

Liking and disliking another human being is no more significant than the fact that some like onions whilst others detest them. There is, however, very great significance in how we handle this. For here we are dealing with a fundamental law. If I permit a very natural dislike to determine my attitude and action towards another person, i.e., if I foster that dislike and confirm it by negative actions towards them, my dislike will certainly increase, and if I persist in this hatred will almost inevitably follow. On the other hand if I act towards another in kindness and concern then my natural antipathy will certainly diminish, for I have opened a door to the flow of *agape* between us and *agape* brings transformation to the human condition. Other people gradually cease to be the problem at the centre of my life.

MEDITATION EXERCISE

REFLECTION

Our reflection is upon the love of God, yet it is beyond the capacity of the human mind to comprehend, 'For the love of God is broader than the measures of man's mind and the heart of the eternal is most wonderfully kind' (*Hymns Ancient and Modern*). We recall the assertion made at the beginning of our journey that 'to fully realise our humanity is to touch divinity'. In the words of the Qur'an, 'He is nearer than our jugular vein'. So it is not with a reaching out into the void that I begin to experience *agape* but as I acknowledge that this love is as close to me as my very breathing.

Need I ask, then, for His presence? The yearning of the heart to know is in itself a calling upon Him. We may do this in the words of a well loved invocation:

> *God be in my head and in my understanding*
> *God be in my eyes and in my looking*
> *God be in my mouth and in my speaking*
> *God be in my heart and in my thinking*
> *God be at mine end and at my departing.*

IMAGINATION

Already we have used our imagination to create representative images of reality along the path, and as we travel on we do so with the knowledge that the light is ever dispelling the darkness and that, however intense, it can never overcome it.

INTUITION

I now go through the pattern of preparation, relaxing the body and centring first of all in body consciousness, then moving on to awareness of allowing the light to permeate my whole body.

With my every breath I take in the light and on my out-breathing send out *agape*.

9

Illusion and Reality

Seek him in the placeless, he will sign you to place: When you seek him in place, he will flee to the placeless. As the arrow speeds from the bow, like the bird of your imagination, know that the Absolute will certainly flee from the imaginary. I will flee from this and that, not for weariness but for fear that my gracious beauty will flee from this and that.

DIVANI SHAMSI TABRIZ, *Selected Poems*
(C.U.P., 1952, first edn. 1898)

It will be seen from our journey so far that the contemplative's perception of life and people is different from those whose primary awareness is at the level of personality interaction and sensual awareness. In fact, we find as we progress along the road that our understanding of what constitutes the real and what is illusion is in process of fundamental change. We see what we have not seen before and hear that which was beyond our capacity to detect. Values change. Instead of judging exclusively by the sight of our eyes and hearing only with our ears, the previously unrecognised comes into clear focus.

Already we have looked at the call to stand at points of intersection between apparently contradictory worlds. We have also to understand that we live in both worlds and, to the extent that we are genuinely seeing with the eye of the heart, to that extent can we live at home in the world of the senses without being dominated and controlled by it.

As a corollary to our newly developed capacity to see beyond the veils or behind the scenes presented by superficial façades is the discovery of the unexpected.

At a conference entitled 'The Displacement of Religion' I was approached by a middle-aged man who asked if he could share with me what he described as 'an exciting new discovery' which had come to him as a result of following a contemplative path. In order to do this it had seemed to him at the time essential that he severed links with the religious institution to which he had belonged since adolescence. This he did, and not without considerable condemnation of what he then regarded as 'a worldwide counterfeit of true spirituality'. 'I determined,' he said, 'to leave it all behind me and make a clean break.' Years later in a nostalgic state of mind he found himself with his family sharing again in the old familiar acts of worship. 'It was all exactly as it had been many years before as far as ritual and externals were concerned. Yet somehow it was quite different. There was still much that intellectually I could not accept but now I could see the real beneath the surface and I resonated with a movement of what I could only describe as "Divine Love" reaching out to me, and to my even greater surprise I knew this to be coming from many of those I had previously dismissed with contempt.'

It is easy to hold to the theory that the mystical experience transcends the theological differences which separate religious bodies. Experiential wisdom takes us beyond theory and in the most surprising situations will find itself demolishing the barriers, discovering reality where previously there was only illusion.

As I listened to this man's story I was reminded of a visit I had recently paid to a famous Buddhist temple in Bangkok. As I entered this vast building I was immediately confronted with symbols and signs and sounds which were unfamiliar to one educated in a quite different and apparently alien religion. The temple was dominated by a huge statue of the Lord Buddha. Around the walls were a number of votive shrines whilst from behind a large screen came the sound of chanting monks. As I looked and thought on what I saw, all seemed unreal and pointing to confusion. I knelt down and closed my eyes to the representations of what to a devout Buddhist were realities well understood. And as I entered into the atmosphere in which the temple was soaked I became aware that it was that of the 'Light, love and power' which the ritual of my own religious training daily verbally affirmed. The illusion of separateness was dispelled.

Extra-sensory perception

Yet this unity has its counterfeit and of this we need to be aware. In the book *The Pilgrim's Progress* written by John Bunyan in the seventeenth century the pilgrim is seen to face the possibility of attractive alternative paths, culs-de-sac of illusion. As a result he would find himself wandering in bypath meadows. From here he would eventually have to return to the straight path.

Such meadows are represented as subtle alternatives to walking in unity with 'the people of the way'. These have their modern counterparts. In recent years many non-verbal types of communication have been uncovered, investigated and developed. They are generally described as 'extra-sensory', for they operate through other than normal sensory channels. Telepathic communication between human beings and between animals and humans is now a well established though still little understood fact. Plants are known to respond and react to human conditions and attitudes.

All such areas of occult activity are to be accounted for by concentration of thought and the operation of metaphysical law that 'energy follows thought'. In most instances such communications are spontaneous and attempts to reproduce them at will are not uniformly successful.

The energies by which the phenomena are brought into operation may be described as horizontal, i.e., consciously exercised; they are in the control of the human ego. Such extra-sensory perceptions may accompany the path of the mystic. Nevertheless they neither validate nor do they spring from mystical consciousness.

Psychic awareness

Closely allied to extra-sensory perception is the area of psychic activity. We need to look at this in some detail, for many who today are looking for clarity in their spiritual journey are unclear as to the distinction between psychic and spiritual. This confusion has been heightened by the frequent juxtaposition of the words psychic and mystic. The two are fundamentally different.

The word psychic requires some definition. It derives from the Greek word *psyche* or soul, a word which in the English language has a great variety of interpretations. People are said to be psychic who allegedly have the ability to see into and to make conscious contact with dimensions beyond the reach of the five senses. Such people are sometimes said to have a sixth sense. The world into which such seeing penetrates is also believed to be that of departed spirits.

As already stated, psychic awareness and mystical perception are quite different. Psychic awareness is an instinctual activity and a residue from an earlier stage of human evolution. The mystic's perception is that of the intuition of the awakened heart.

The third quarter of the nineteenth century in the Western world witnessed the rise of great interest in psychic phenomena, and in the year 1882 an organisation was founded in Great Britain called the Society for Psychic Research. Its purpose was said to be as follows: 'To investigate various alleged phenomena apparently inexplicable by known laws of nature and commonly referred to by Spiritualists as the agency of extra-terrestrial intelligences.'

In the mid-1950s, acting under increasing pressure within the churches for 'explanations of psychic phenomena', 'The Churches Fellowship for Spiritual and Psychical Studies' was formed. This had as its aim the evaluation of the mounting claims of those who appeared to be in touch with the energies of the psychic world, and particularly those claiming to be in touch with the departed.

With the great release of energy that came about in the 1960s there has been a marked proliferation of psychic activity. Psychic power emanates from the emotional centre of the human being and, in my experience, when there is an intense build-up of emotional energy psychic forces are released.

During my days of ministry in the English Midlands I held office as a Diocesan Exorcist. One one occasion I was called in to 'clean up' a house where psychic phenomena, such as noises and bangings of every description, were causing considerable distress to the inhabitants. Enquiry quickly revealed, to the great surprise of the inhabitants, that the trouble began as the result of an all-night prayer meeting. As the praying proceeded, emotional tension increased to the point of almost frenzied anxiety. The proceedings were focussed upon the lady of the house whom it was believed was 'possessed' by an evil spirit. Clearly the prayer meeting itself had been the cause of the disturbance. The sustained and frenzied petitioning of the Almighty through the long hours of the night had generated within the petitioners themselves a very high level of emotional energy. This, coupled with the considerable anxiety of the lady of the house, already in a highly neurotic state, had produced changes of consciousness amongst many of those present, to the extent that they saw and heard things normally beyond human perception.

How are we to evaluate the significance of psychic activities?

Psychic activity is not to be dismissed, in the manner of some, as the work of the devil or, on the other hand, to be glamorised into a spiritual awakening. Psychic ability in itself is neither good nor bad, and must be judged by the uses to which it is put. As power in the hands of egocentric people it may be the means of an unhealthy control over others. But only those who give such alleged powers place, space and recognition are susceptible. No psychic powers can touch us unless there lies within us a ready resonance.

Astral, psychic and emotional

The psychic world is created by the aggregate of human emotions. If we think in three-dimensional terms, it exists as a layer or band encircling the earth, operating between that of the physical and spiritual world. So we may visualise the terrestrial world at the centre, surrounded and enveloped by the emotional world, and these two worlds held within the context of the spiritual world. All this can, of course, be internalised, but for the purpose of simple visualisation we may see it in this way.

The world of the emotions in occult terminology is called the astral world, so we may take astral, psychic and emotional as having one meaning. This was brought powerfully into human consciousness by Theosophy and Anthroposophy at the beginning of this century.

How is the reality of this world affirmed? It is as objectively real as our emotions. To the extent that our emotions exist and in the measure that we give them space, to that extent is the astral world real. This it is important to be aware of. In other words it has as much reality as we are prepared to give to it. If experientially (as distinct from theoretically) we refuse it recognition, then it has no objective existence.

How is this world created and renewed? Throughout our lifespan we are all involved in this process. This is effected through our behaviour patterns, relationships and the exercise of our wills. The astral world is thus shaped and recreated. Although of necessity we are using the language of time and space, this world relates primarily to a fourth dimension.

There is unceasing interplay between the astral and the physical worlds, for whilst the astral realm is the creation of human beings it in turn powerfully influences human behaviour, both individually and collectively. It is a world of powerful thought forms to which what the Christian Scriptures call 'natural' man is exposed and by which he is shaped. Currents of energy from this world flow unceasingly into the uncontrolled human psyche, determining the behaviour patterns of the human race to an extraordinary degree. It is also a world which is created and uncreated through conflict, as we saw in the imagery of the human shadow in Chapter 8. Here the unregulated flow of negative forces creates a world of destructive power, a world which is subservient only to the highest of human energies, that of *agape*.

There is an occult saying that 'As above so below'. We may see this in the relationship between the physical and astral worlds. When consciousness is released from the physical body by death, like calls to like and it gravitates to its 'rightful place'. The substance of the personality belongs to the astral world. Shaped and fashioned at the level of the physical, it now returns to source where the stripping of the unreal from the real takes place. Where personality existed apart from the true essence it feels itself to be entirely at home and at rest. The 'real' or spiritual core of the human being is drawn irresistibly to its Source beyond astral consciousness.

Survival after death

Is there a valid and validated conscious relationship between physical beings and those centres of consciousness in the astral world? May we look in that direction for help and support as we follow the straight path? This depends upon what exactly we are looking for. If we feel the need to be assured that there is such a thing as survival of the personality beyond the death of the body, then the 'evidence' provided by those who believe they have established such contact can give the reassurance sought for.

Since the end of the last century a vast amount of such evidence has been accumulated by mediums and those known as sensitives, to indicate that emotions in the shape of human personalities do survive beyond the grave. Even allowing for deception and delusion the evidence is impressive. What is important to realise is that survival of the emotions and personality is not what is to be understood by immortality. Immortality concerns what we have called the essence of the human being and is a state of being as far removed from human cognition as is the human being from the senses of the insect. The astral or emotional dimension does not take us entirely beyond time, and the corruption which inevitably overtakes all physical matter must ultimately consume the emotional substance in the non-physical world. This constitutes the 'second death'.

Transition from the body to the next stage of human existence, whilst it does consist of and apparently provides evidence for an after-life, is something quite distinct from immortality – which we shall examine in the next chapter.

The question which the contemplative must ask is, 'Would such communion with the departed aid growth into maturity in this life?' All valid aids, whether from this physical sphere or from any other, throw us back upon our own potential. This was the point where our journey began and this must always be our touchstone.

Reincarnation

Closely allied to concepts relating to the 'after-life' are those to do with belief in reincarnation. And here we remind ourselves that the path we are following is concerned not with beliefs but with knowledge of the heart. Beliefs of all kinds are the crystallisation of a dynamic and it is this inner truth which we endeavour to touch in our examination of the subject. First we must look briefly at what is understood by the word.

Of all the five great world religions two, i.e., Hinduism and

Buddhism, teach reincarnation as articles of faith. But there is no simple single theory held in common of what exactly reincarnates into matter. According to Hinduism it is the ego or indestructable self which repeatedly assumes form in this life. Buddhists have no doctrine of an individual self or ego. For them it is forms of consciousness which reincarnate, though it is left undefined as to whether the plurality of consciousness represented by each sentient being has any kind of separate identity.

The inner truth at the heart of these theories of what exactly constitutes reincarnation is that consciousness in some form or other is indestructible. As in the physical world, release into higher forms is achieved by the transmuting of energy. This is the evolutionary process by which the human and the Divine find union. The reverse process is disintegration. Nothing in the universe of matter remains static. Doctrinal definitions of this inevitably create divisions, diversity and separation. In previous ages this has been desirable and even necessary in order to preserve identity within separated cultures and societies. With the growth of a one-world consciousness and the birth of a spirituality centred in experiential wisdom it is now important to rediscover the essence of truth behind diversity of forms, for herein lies essential unity and unity of the essence!

To move in this direction is to cease thinking in terms of past and future and through penetrative (intuitive) rather than linear thought – to which theories of reincarnation belong – discover the meaning of the present moment, and so to move beyond belief.

TWELVE POINTERS ALONG THE CONTEMPLATIVE PATH

We noted earlier the possibility, and for some of us the probability, of diverting from the straight path into bypath meadows. In the context of a profusion of beliefs and pressures to follow many paths, are there terms of reference by which we may travel with confidence? There are no textbook answers, but there are clear guideposts. Here are twelve pointers along the contemplative path.

1. LEARN TO GIVE AND TO RECEIVE

Be childlike in your capacity to receive, and allow for growth within your own understanding. You are on a journey and today's staging post can easily become a cul-de-sac. Respect all knowledge whilst remembering that controversy never gives birth to spiritual growth. Point-scoring does nothing but inflate the ego. Acknowledge to yourself the capacity to see where reality lies, but with this cultivate the ability to be silent. It is not your responsibilty to bring into the open another's secrets, rather is it your duty to give unobtrusive support.

2. IN YOUR STABILITY BE FLEXIBLE

Remember that your illusion may be another's reality. It is not for you to undermine or to denigrate. However much we may feel we understand about others we can never see the whole picture, nor can we know with certainty the path another needs to take. All must answer for themselves. Because it has seemed right and comfortable for you to express your experience of the inner life in a particular way, do not assume that this is the only form it can take. Leave wide open the possibility that for the sake of others you may need to articulate your truth in a different manner.

3. FOLLOW THE MIDDLE WAY

An Italian proverb says 'See all things, turn away from most, try to put a few things right!' Sometimes you may feel yourself called to reform society. Do not make the mistake of thinking that you can change everything. The greatest reforms have emanated from men and women whose 'beingness' acted as a catalyst.

Never be too proud to say 'I do not understand', or 'this is beyond my capacity to grasp'. Humility on your part may give faith to another.

Learn to hear where the questions are coming from and listen to your answers.

4. LEARN TO DISCRIMINATE WITHOUT JUDGING

Every challenging situation, every demanding circumstance is the very opportunity you need to prove the stability of the path you are pursuing. Your path may not be that followed by those close to you. Each person must follow the beat of the drum that they hear. See clearly that the meditative pattern you are following in your set-apart times is a focussing of the humdrum of daily living. You cannot fit your pattern into that worn by others. One person's comfortable and enabling dress is another's strait-jacket. Concede to all others their full right to believe and to know as they will, and at the same time *maintain your own space*. Stand on the hill of clear perspectives.

5. LEARN TO AVOID FOLLOWING THE PROJECTIONS OF PERSONAL DESIRE

If oppressed by heat and thirst, the desert traveller may easily become strongly convinced that salvation is on the horizon. A camp, an oasis, whatever is at the heart of a desperately felt need, appears in the form of a mirage. These are no more than a projection of personal desire. There is a wise saying, 'All holy desires grow by delays, and if they don't then they are not holy.' The personal does not necessarily have to be denied. It has to be held within the context of the greater good. To race after a personal mirage may lead to an immediate emotional satisfaction. It will almost inevitably lead through the mirage into turbulence.

6. RESIST INTRUSION AND DO NOT INTRUDE

Remember the Greetings Dance! When pressed emotionally, then is the time to step aside. Not all circumstances of pressure and potential stress can be dealt with whilst remaining within the situation. Recognise when it is time to stand back. The personality of another may clearly appear to you as nothing more than a mask. That does not give you the right to violate it. Closer contact is permissible only in response to invitation. You too may claim the right to hide or play a role, provided you are clear about the reason why.

7. TRUST YOURSELF TO KNOW THE ANSWERS

Scriptures, spiritual books, inspirational talks of every kind, gurus and teachers all have a function at the right time and place, to reflect back to you that which is 'dawning in your own mind'. Beyond that they merely add to the ceaseless function of informing the intellect.

Everyday occurrences, ordinary circumstances and casual acquaintances all have their place in holding before you the mirror of reality. This may happen when you are invited to respond to another's quest for meaning and a sense of direction. You too, if you will trust yourself, may in that moment reflect the answer. Such a response on your part, if from the heart, will meet the need at a far deeper level than would all the 'authorities' in the world. The paradox is that the one who is enquiring will be answering their own question. Learn to trust yourself.

8. NEVER ANSWER QUESTIONS THAT ARE NOT BEING ASKED

An otherwise efficient and delightful secretary had the confusing habit, when she did not know the answer to a specific question, of replying immediately with an eloquent burst of totally irrelevant information. As her employer I was effectively mentally paralysed by such a response. Remember that words are not the primary level of enquiry, neither are they the first level of response. 'Truth' when verbalised may quickly become a weapon. And at that point the contemplative becomes a propagandist!

9. FIND THE KEY TO MEANING IN THE ORDINARY

Your present life lived out on the planet is central to understanding the fundamental principles of the spiritual life. The extraordinary lies at the heart of the ordinary. It is not to be found in trips or kicks created by experimental excursions into emotional ecstasies. Rather, such experiments cause us to become at first fascinated, then bewildered and finally confused as the cloud of delusion envelops us. Life's secrets are hidden in the present moment wherever that happens to be. The colourful flowers of 'other-worldly' experiences may look and smell delightful. To go after them invariably means wandering in bypass meadow.

10. CULTIVATE AND CHERISH RELATIONSHIPS

To preserve your individual integrity does not mean isolation. The contemplative path has many pilgrims. You are one of the 'people of the way', part of a vast network of Light encircling the globe, as we realise in our meditation. Within this understanding, cultivate a right estimate of yourself. Again you are living within a paradox. You are not the centre of the universe, yet you are central to its wholeness. Your spiritual awareness has a vital place within the Divine plan and purpose for the planet, yet everything does not depend on your spiritual evolution.

The awakened heart has a magnetic attraction. This operates in self-forgetfulness. Other forms of attraction involve manipulation and possessiveness. This is not your way. Remember that you have far more friends than you will ever be aware of, more people working for your greater good than you can imagine, and true friendship will come when you are least looking for it and when you need it most. Look, and without doubt sooner or later you will become aware of others walking with you along the path.

11. BEGIN THE JOURNEY AFRESH EACH DAY

'When should I have my period of meditation?' is a question frequently asked. There is no proper time and no correct place. If the contemplative way were possible only for those with suitable places and those who could relate to suitable times, then the mystic would belong to an elitist group unrelated to the vicissitudes of the greater varieties of lifestyles common to the human species.

Look at the daily rhythm of your life, and within the pattern of that rhythm have a starting point. Morning, noon or night, your circumstances, your metabolism and your will will determine your starting point. It is unlikely that either the climate or daily responsibilities will permit you to pitch a tent in the desert or enable you to escape into the forest. An occasional retreat may not be impossible. It would be easy to say with Shakespeare that 'the readiness is all', but that would be unrealistic. Establish starting points as you are able and from wanderings in wide-open spaces so return again and again to the straight path knowing (paradoxically) that each time you are a little further on.

12. DON'T HESITATE TO TURN YOUR ANGER UPON GOD

You are a fully human being, and desirable as it undoubtedly is to transmute and consciously direct all your emotional energies, it is both realistic and wise to anticipate those occasions when they break through their boundaries. It is then healthy to bring God into the equation, allowing the blast of your anger and frustration to be directed to the Source from whom we may reasonably expect our help to come! Whatever image or imagelessness you hold of the Deity, to face this in your time of need will without doubt foster the healing of wounds and bring control without repression. It is of the very essence of God that He/She is vulnerable and responsive to your need, even when you feel at your lowest ebb.

MEDITATION EXERCISE

REFLECTION

Along the way I have encountered many new aspects of humanity – my humanity. The journey began with an acknowledgement of my 'total humanness', all of which is to be accepted. I now reflect upon the fact that there is one life-giving force which operates in all human beings. This force, this energy is capable of manifesting in a great diversity of ways and at many levels of human experience.

I have chosen to bring this creative energy to a single point-edness of purpose. This is the significance of 'heart centred-ness'. This is a process which requires that I constantly choose this way as that to which I have commited my life. This does not preserve me from mistakes nor from the ever-present possibility of self-deception. It does assure me of an ever-readiness to return to the centre where I renew my sights and offer up my energy to be one with the Divine plan and purpose for my life and that of all humanity. This is the very *raison d'être* of my meditation.

IMAGINATION

The road ahead is as I have always perceived it to be, straight and clear. As I have already observed, there is a two-way movement, i.e., of people leaving and joining the path. Some leave for a time and then return, and with their movement is also the movement of the Light. I observe that for those who are joining the path, whether for the first time or after a departure, the Light itself never leaves them, and it is warm and welcoming.

INTUITION

I move through the stages of relaxation and body-consciousness to once again centring in the heart. I allow myself time to be still, both externally and within, and now become aware that the Light not only rises within me but that the Light is pouring down upon me, into my body, from above. To this down-pouring of Light I relate my inbreathing. On my inbreath I bring in the Light from above. On my outbreathing I radiate the Light, and without strain or tension allow the all-permeating Light to flow in and to flow out.

I affirm and close my meditation with the words:

'God is Light and in Him is no darkness at all.'

10

Between Two Worlds

To some outraged spirits, no doubt, man appeared diminished and dethroned by this evolutionary theory which made him no more than the latest arrival in the animal kingdom. But to the minds of the majority our human condition seemed finally to be exalted by the fact that we were rooted in the fauna and soil of the planet . . . evolving man in the forefront of the animals.

PIERRE TEILHARD DE CHARDIN , *Phenomenon of Man*
(Fontana, 1983)

In following the path of experiential wisdom our primary concern has been to establish signposts which point the way forward along the straight path. It is important that we now place the journey into a wider context and pose the question How does a contemplative understanding perceive and relate to life on this planet as we enter the twenty-first century?

One of the marked characteristics of the age in which we live is that, in spite of the forces of separativeness working in society, it is increasingly difficult for human beings to live in separate boxes, whether such boxes be created by patterns of thought or modes of living. The day when groups of people could without too much difficulty adhere to an exclusive way of life or set pattern of beliefs, and preserve them from erosion from within or irresistible pressure from without, is rapidly passing. Anyone who has reached middle life towards the end of the twentieth century can look within the limits of their own experience and be acutely aware of this process of erosion and pressure.

Added to this is the rapidity of change, for in the latter half of the century the speed of change has exceeded any comparable period of recorded history. Even in the realms of advanced technology yesterday's advance in human inventiveness is today's historical curiosity. The result has been an intense and mounting emotional and mental pressure upon large sections of the human race. Since the Second World War over one hundred acknowledged wars have broken out and the vision of world peace seems as remote as ever. The human race appears to be caught up in a vortex of uncontrollable and unpredictable energies, thrusting humanity towards – who can tell – destruction or re-creation?

Until the late 1980s the shape of the world and its inhabitants was perceived as the Western nations, the Eastern bloc and the Third World. All this has crumbled. In the context of powerfully emerging human aspirations from within, these structures have become demonstrably unreal, superimposed and therefore superficial, unrelated to those factors ethnic, cultural and religious – which create a real cohesiveness in society. So we are experiencing volcanic-like eruptions from within, and beneath all this may be perceived a universal struggle for identity, a struggle which, for those with eyes to see, may yet be recognised as presaging a crucial new chapter in the long history of human evolution. A leading Western politician at the end of a public lecture on the state of the nation cried out to his audience: 'I want only to turn my back on the future.'

What has become increasingly clear is that there is no inevitability of progress, for what is also manifest is that in the short term human destiny is within human hands. What could emerge, and appears to be already breaking into world consciousness, is that there is not one grouping, one corpus of political dogma, no one religious body and, above all, no superhuman individual able to provide a solution to the human dilemma of how to avoid self-destruction and promote a future for the human being in its totality. That this perception is growing is good, but its emergence is of itself insufficient, for unless it is informed by and consciously linked to that very dimension from which it takes its authentic origin, it will inevitably founder on anxiety, generated by frustration, and will end in despair.

As we have already seen, there are today many movements ostensibly endeavouring to effect change, born of goodwill yet of a potentially violent nature. That these campaigns sometimes operate under the banner of 'consciousness-raising' is irony indeed! Such movements are often instigated by those who have a passionate concern to 'save the world'. Their vision is of a unified humanity. It is indeed in part an holistic vision. All too often this proves to be an isolated idealism – isolated, that is, from the spiritual impulse and empowerment without which it must inevitably turn in upon itself, so generating further discord and harmony. And such impulses cannot be realised nor released without self-discipline. One is reminded of the words of Nurse Edith Cavell, executed in the First World War for aiding prisoners of war: 'Patriotism is not enough . . .'. In this context we may turn them into 'Idealism is not enough'. The desire to reform, if allied only to anger, carries with it the seeds of self-destruction.

Impulses towards wholeness

Yet, in spite of such apparent failure in so many areas, there is today on a universal scale an undoubted powerful impulse towards wholeness manifesting within the human psyche – something more than isolated idealism. As we follow the contemplative path we are concerned with the recognition of and relating to this impulse.

As we have followed this path so we have from time to time reminded ourselves that the journey in which we are taking part is very much more than an individual pursuit, followed apart from society as a whole and disregarding the great movements of history which shape human destiny. To be concerned with your own spiritual growth and evolution is to be giving yourself, in co-operation with all impulses operating towards humanity's greater good and the realising of the vision of wholeness. Yet the work of transformation and re-creation must begin within you. This is where rebirth and renewal begins.

Jesus of Nazareth was once visited secretly by a well known teacher of divinity to whom he declared, 'You must be born again', i.e., you must go through the process of re-creation in order to live in what will prove to be the real world! Intellectually and religiously perplexed, Nicodemus countered with, 'How can these things be?' Jesus replied, 'The new birth is like the movement of the wind.' Its origins and progression are beyond detection. Yet its effects are felt and known. Rebirth and entrance into the 'real' world takes place as we allow the winds of change to operate within.

Contemplative concerns for the twenty-first century

So far we have used the terms mystic and contemplative inter-changeably, but in looking at today's needs and the contemporary situation we may perceive a distinction between the function of those traditionally known as mystics and today's contemplatives. Experientially the mystic and the contemplative are one. Both recognise the mystery of the unity of all things. Both are concerned to relate to this mystery. In essence they are one, yet today's contemplative has a distinctive function, a conscious role in society. The late twentieth-century contemplative is concerned to relate mystical awareness to a philosophy which embraces the whole of life, and to new concepts of time and space.

We have referred to positive and creative impulses within society, movements of convergence. At the centre of these is the realisation – albeit a reluctant one for many to whom conscious contemplation is a closed book – that the mystery not only of planet earth but the universe itself cannot be entered into exclusively through the five senses.

This has been brought into stark focus through the exploration of space. The limits of such exploration are set by the lifespan of the human being. Even a hundred years of travel could represent no more than the crossing of the threshold. Linear exploration has immutable limits fixed by the ageing process. Orthodox scientific advance is now entering a cul-de-sac and science fiction is increasingly preoccupied with transcending the limitations imposed by time and space.

Today both science and religion are being pressed towards a reassessment of what exactly constitutes the fully human being. Are there dimensions and faculties as yet unrealised? And will a contemplative philosophy contribute to a new understanding of these potentials?

As long ago as 1905 new vistas of possibility were opened up when Albert Einstein propounded his theory of relativity. This was to lead physics to abandon the Newtonian theory of absolute time and absolute space. A journey inward had begun. Inherent in Einstein's thinking was the conviction that space and time and the laws of motion can be defined only in reference to the condition of the observer. Suddenly the scientific observer had become like the mystic or the contemplative, part of the world which was being observed. The scientist himself had become part of the world of physics.

In more recent times the scientist Michin Kaku has said in his book *Hyperspace* (O.U.P., 1994):

> *I think one of the deepest experiences a scientist can have, almost approaching a religious awakening, is to realise that we are children of the stars, and that our minds are capable of understanding its Universal Laws that they obey. The atoms in our bodies were forged on the anvil of nucleo-synthesis within an exploding star aeons before the birth of the solar system. Our atoms are older than the mountains. We are literally made of stardust. Now these atoms have in time coalesced into intelligent human beings*

capable of understanding its universal laws governing the events.
We have the same laws on our tiny planet as there are everywhere
in the universe.

Here, approached from within the scientific disciplines, is an
expression of that essential unity at the heart of mystical understanding. Each of one substance, the observed and the observer
become one.

The cosmologist Stephen Hawking (quoted in *Hyperspace*,
p. 334) has said:

> *If we do discover a complete theory, it should in time be under-*
> *standable in broad principle by everyone, not just a few scientists.*
> *Then we shall all, philosophers, scientists and just ordinary peo-*
> *ple, be able to take part in the discussion of the question of why it*
> *is that we and the universe exist. If we find the reason to that it*
> *will be the ultimate triumph of reason . . . for then we should*
> *know the mind of God.*

Hawking makes two very significant points in this statement,
i.e., that a 'complete theory' would be understood by everyone, and that this would ultimately lead to knowing 'the mind
of God'. What we might question is whether this would be the
'triumph of reason' or that of another aspect of the human
mind!

It is this acknowledgement of the wholeness and interrelat-
edness of all Creation, and where human beings are seen to be
an integral and essential part of Creation, that modern scientific
development may be said to be running parallel to the direction
being taken by today's contemplatives. Yet it is important to
distinguish between the perceptions of science and those of the
contemplative. The new physics, I suggest, are now demonstrating the relativity of time and space and bringing us to new
vistas of reality which take us beyond both. Further scientific
progress may bring us to at present undreamed-of revelations.
The recognition of essential links between the observer and the

observed is now a recognition that consciousness both pervades and extends beyond matter, thus bringing the concept of mind within scientific cognition. Yet we need to be clear that it is only that consciousness which proceeds from human acquiescence with the Divine Will, i.e., what we have called centring in the heart, which can respond and relate to that ultimate reality we call God and all that is packed into that word. No scientific investigation nor progress can give birth of itself to this level of understanding. Extension of human consciousness 'beyond' what we know of the physical universe, or the establishment of rapport within new dimensions, may be no more than a refined form of scientific materialism.

New realisations of reality

I have no doubt from the response I have received from groups and communities in many parts of the world that the concept (and increasingly more than a concept) of a new realisation of what constitutes objective reality is beginning to enter into human consciousness. To the physical body the physical world is objectively real, to the emotional body the world of emotions – at which we looked in an earlier chapter – is objectively real. And at this stage of human evolution the objectivity of spiritual realities beyond the physical veils is becoming apparent.

This is the dynamic operating within the human being which must eventually lead to the creation of a new map of reality by which the 'people of the way' will learn to live; a map other than that furnished by the contours of the physical world as it has been hitherto known and understood. If this appears to relate only to imaginative flights of fantasy and fancy, let us remind ourselves that this is precisely how Galileo's perspective of the earth and its place in the universe was received, and in our own time the initial vistas of outer space.

All this has to be earthed within ourselves, an expansion of understanding rooted in and stemming from *agape*. And with the widening of our horizons there will be no diminishment of our humanity, no lessening of our participation in all aspects of life. For this is not a superimposing by external influences from above, but rather an eruption of energy from within, the flowering of a new humanity. The authority of relating to the evolutionary impulse will be affirmed as we practise the discipline of undifferentiating seeing. Such seeing is non-selective, not a reflection of human emotions. We are beholding a cosmic unveiling, a mystery reflected in the mirror of the heart, a seeing of things as they are.

At our present stage of awareness and evolution such perceptions come to most as spontaneous unpremeditated realisation. I recall one such happening in my own experience. I was entering a crowded railway station during the evening rush hour. Travellers were arriving from every direction and crowding into the trains. Suddenly it was as if the whole scene changed and for a brief instant I saw beneath the surface of this surging mass of apparent individuals. One moment there were before me and all around hundreds of faces, each one a focal point of a hurrying jostling form. Next the majority of the bodies and faces disappeared. Those remaining appeared as beings of Light, their physical forms no longer visible. The rest merged into a sea of empty expressionless masks, tossing aimlessly in all directions. Then, like the croquet players in *Alice in Wonderland* who collapsed into a pack of cards, they dissolved into nothingness.

We can only speculate as to exactly how the energy we now know as planet earth exploded into time and space. We can know that it has evolved through many phases of manifestation and that this is also true of the forms of life to which it has given birth and nurtured. This process continues.

As we have seen, sensual perception can comprehend only the material world, i.e., the physical manifestations of the planet. The contemplative is aware of its other modes of expression, modes which are not only recognised with the eye of faith but which may be entered into experientially.

The apocalyptic (i.e., the unveiler) looks for a dramatic ending to the world, the contemplative recognises the passing of one world and the revealing of another. The veils are thus penetrated experientially.

In acknowledging this possibility we need to understand that humanity itself is part of the changes which underlie and penetrate all matter. Metamorphosis involves all creation. It follows from this that a true Self-consciousness will give insight into and understanding of the changes which are now taking place and prompt an awakening into further understanding.

The ending of a world and the birth of a new is not to be looked for by physical changes effected from without, but rather by an eruption of life from within. This will have the aspect of a 'leap' from the imprisonment of the space-time continuum, when for those with eyes to see the new world will be open from within.

And look, those far infinities, which for the senses fixed the boundaries
Of the universe, are gone.
They too were shadows
Which with the dawning of the Light
Turn in upon themselves
And with the speed of that same Light,
All are encompassed
In the human heart.

The Omega Vision

So do we enter into immortality. For the contemplative looks not for survival but for transformation, not for an 'after'-life but rather to know reality in the present moment.

This is to surrender to the Light, to be fulfilled by and perfected in *agape*.

The prophetic in the present moment

All who have chosen to be particpants in this cosmic unveiling – and this is fundamental to the contemplative journey – find themselves again functioning within a paradox. The inner journey is by its very nature a secret and hidden way. At every stage the maxim applies, 'Those who know do not tell, those who tell do not know.' It is equally true that from commitment to this journey issues the responsibility for the exercise of a prophetic ministry. Here it is important that we understand the meaning of 'prophetic'.

Against the background of a predominantly Judaeo-Christian history and culture a prophet is not primarily one who foretells the future but rather as a 'forthteller', one who declares 'what is', who expresses the truth of the present moment. The history of the Israelites in the Jewish Scriptures is that of recurring cycles of failure and success, a falling and rising, defect and achievement in response to the Divine call to the nation and to individuals towards wholeness. Again and again the Scriptures record that 'the people of God did evil in the sight of the Lord'. It was when this happened that the Lord sent a prophet to speak to the need and to draw out the potential of His people.

A fascinating account of one such intervention is recorded in the story of Gideon. These events took place at a particularly low point in the fortunes of the nation. Oppressed by surrounding alien tribes who regularly plundered the fruits of their harvest, the people of God despaired of survival. In a situation of apparent futility we see the man Gideon threshing wheat whilst expecting it to be snatched away. Suddenly an angel of the Lord appears. The dramatic nature of the angel's appearance is highlighted by the fact that he is described as 'sitting under an oak tree'. The message he brought to an incredulous

Gideon was strange in the extreme. It was twofold: 'The Lord is with you, mighty man of valour', and 'Go in the strength that you already have'. Gideon went and the Lord went with him.

The development of a prophetic witness is effected not by the proffering of alleged deposits of truth. Still less is it to herald details of a supposed future apocalypse. Rather is it to seek the alignment with the dynamic which unveils the realities of the present moment. To align myself in this way is to enter into a true prophethood.

Atonement and prayer

A word common to many religious vocabularies and theological understandings is that of atonement. For me it is one of the few religious words that remains firmly embodied in my mind since the days of childhood learning. This is for the reason that my religious teacher unwrapped the word for me and explained it – for the sophisticated perhaps naively – as meaning simply 'at-one-ment'. I liked it then and I like it now, for it perfectly describes for me the aligning of the lesser to the greater, the personal to the cosmic, the human to the Divine. To achieve such atonement is the very *raison-d'être* of our meditative disciplines, for the constant and regular reaffirming of that atonement is the way of contemplative prayer. How may we define this process?

Contemplative prayer is first of all an attitude of intuitive awareness. From this it may be seen that in essential content meditation and prayer express one and the same intention. Yet, in the light of a growing vision of meaning and purpose for the whole created order, there comes to birth a yearning to co-operate with all that is contributing to the realisation of this, not only within ourselves but within others. So from awareness to receptivity springs the desire to affirm this all-pervading process wherever it is struggling to manifest. We develop a longing to 'go with the movement' and this may be articulated in a diversity that expresses an essential unity. In the language of the Hindu we may relate in intention to the emergence of the 'true self' within others. With the Buddhist we yearn for humanity to experience Buddhahood, and with the Christian we seek to see and encourage the coming to birth of the Christ-consciousness wherever it may be found.

Such prayer can never be static. The affirmation of that which is already known inevitably leads to a conscious willingness to accept its implications and to work with these implications in terms of the Divine plan and purpose. For prayer cannot change the Divine will. Rather does it release it into our consciousness.

Towards a wider dimension

We need now to take an overview of our journey and the wider dimensions implicit within contemplative awareness. To do this requires that we again use our imagination, capacity for reflection and intuitive perception, and experience this as a meditation.

In our mind's eye we are aware of the origin of all things. This we see and feel as a vast explosion of energy manifesting in time and space as matter. The source of this is that which we call 'God'. Yet the source is not to be conceived as detached and separate from that to which it gives birth and which proceeds from it.

Inherent therefore in the world of matter and also existing as the sustainer, God both contains and is contained by this creation, though He is not to be identified with it.

The stream of energy expanding outwards from the Source gives birth to multiplicity of form, forms which are constantly being shaped and reshaped. The life force operating within these forms is always seeking to draw the essence back to the Source itself. The former action is that of creation, the latter that of evolution.

The world of matter and form thus becomes the means by which the Divine life seeks to express itself, first through multiplicity of form, then by drawing altogether into the one. This twofold action is effected through struggle and suffering, for every form of matter contains not only potential for union with the whole, a resonance with the magnetic pull to return to source, but also a capacity for a kind of completion within itself, a circle of existence separate from the whole and therefore of temporal duration. Such a separated circle of existence becomes in effect a short circuit, an individualisation rejecting its part in the whole.

It is this capacity for and inclination towards separation, this will for self-destruction, that the Divine love is ever seeking to nullify, identifying itself with all forms of manifestation and seeking to lift all into oneness. Writ large across the whole scenario is the process of birth, life, death and the possibility of resurrection.

The spearhead of the movement to integrate within the whole is created and operated by awakened human beings, the people of the way. They are awakened because, aware of life impulses striving to operate in and through them, they have awakened to the reality of a powerful and regenerative force, personal yet all-embracing. With this they have freely chosen to co-operate. They have become – whether they know it or not, and regardless of labels self-applied or given by others – men and women of prayer.

Put in another way, it is as if all the ingredients or essential parts of a Divine plan embracing time and space and all that is contained therein, are embodied within the created order, but without a conscious 'yes' from the heart of humanity the myriad parts cannot coalesce or come together, the shape of the whole cannot emerge. It is this 'yes' from the human heart that contains all the elements of true prayer. Without this co-operation the impulse towards cohesion and meaning is unable to do more than pulsate within confined spheres. Each level of consciousness within creation remains a world turned in upon itself, affecting no more than a physical life span. Such an understanding of prayer gives meaning and purpose to all life. It does no violence to the intellect and is in accordance with the scientific recognition of all matter as a manifestation of energy. It is a bringing together of two worlds.

Appendix

BASIC MEDITATIONAL EXERCISE

Intention The intention of meditation is to discover and relate to the still centre within, that is the heart. These exercises may be used by individuals or groups.

STEPS TO TAKE

The body The first step concerns the physical body. The aim is to find a position which combines relaxation and alertness. For most people this means sitting in a straight-backed chair. The head should be held erect, the hands clasped loosely in the lap or placed palms flat against the thighs, and the feet against the floor or tucked beneath the chair. This position can be modified according to individual needs. What is important is that as far as possible the position of the body should express the intention of the meditator. The physical form thus becomes an outward sign of an inner state of being, that is of relaxed alertness.

The breath The body is now in position and we are ready to follow a process of relaxation. It is helpful to relate this to breathing. This is done systematically. Begin with the head and on the out-breath relax the scalp and facial muscles. Do the same with the shoulders, arms, waist, thighs, legs and feet. Finally breathe out several times as though through all the pores of the body, consciously relaxing the whole physical frame. If you become aware of the tightening up of any muscles, return to that part and again consciously relax. Take this slowly.

Observation With the mind's eye now observe your body, relaxed yet alert. Reverence your body, that is accept it as a unique God-given vehicle of the real you.

The emotions Allow yourself to become aware of your emotions. They too constitute a body. Unlike the physical body it is not confined in one limited space. It is immensely 'busy' in many areas. Allow yourself to become aware of any areas of emotional tension. Do not try to deal with or repress them. Recognise them; observe, acknowledge and let them go. As with the physical body, the process of stepping back from emotional tension may be related to the breathing, so on each out-breath let go of the pressures and the tensions.

The intellect The uncontrolled activity of the intellect blocks off true awareness. As with the emotions, so with the intellect – we need to distance ourselves, to step back from the incessant chatter of the brain. To 'try' to do this can be self-defeating. Allow the mind gradually to quieten down. Gently allow it to relate to one thing. So gradually bring the attention to the centre of the chest and allow it to focus there.

The still centre We are now identifying the heart of our being. This is the still centre, the place of 'perfect clear perception'.

Refocusing If and when the attention wanders, as you become aware of this, so gently return to the focal point and centre again. Remember it is the 'intention' that matters. Each return to the centre reinforces this.

Visualisation The concept of light is basic. The Light has the qualities both of peace and love. It is that described in the New Testament as the Light of the World.

Two points to remember

1. The Light is always present within the heart.
2. Centred in this Light, you are always in complete control.

Bibliography

Bennett, J.G., *The Dramatic Universe*, Combe Springs, 1960

Bunyan, John, *Pilgrim's Progress*, Hodder, 1988

Blakeney, Dr R.B. (translator), *The Way of Life: Tao Te Ching* by Lao Tzu, New American Library, 1955

de Chardin, Father Pierre Teilhard, *Phenomenon of Man*, Fontana, 1983

Franck, Frederick, *The Zen of Seeing*, Wildwood House, 1973

Gibran, Khahil, *The Phrophet*, Heinemann, 1926

Griffiths, Dom Bede, *The Universal Christ*, Darton, Longman and Todd, 1990

Gurdjieff, George Ivanovitch, *All and Everything: Meetings with Remarkable Men*, Penguin, 1990

Happold, F.C., *Religious Faith and Twentieth Century Man*, Darton, Longman and Todd, new edn. 1980, *The Journey Inward*, Darton, Longman and Todd, 1968

Huxley, Aldous, *The Perennial Philosophy*, Chatto and Windus, 1980

James, William, *The Varieties of Religious Experience*, Penguin, new edn. 1983

Kaku, Michin, *Hyperspace*, O.U.P., 1994

Macaulay, Rose, *The Towers of Trebizond*, Fontana, 1990

Phillips, J.B., *Your God Is Too Small*, Wyvern Press, 1956

Robinson, John, *Honest to God*, SCM Press, 1956

Scholem, Gershom, *Major Trends of Jewish Mysticism*, Schocken Books, 1949

Shah, Idris, *The Sufis*, Octagon Press, 1964

Spink, Peter, *The Christian in The New Age*, Darton, Longman and Todd, 1991, *The End of An Age*, Darton, Longman and Todd, 1983

Stace, W.T., *The Teachings of the Mystics*, New American Library, 1960

Steiner, Rudolf, *An Outline of Occult Science*, Rudolf Steiner Press, 1964

Tabriz, Divani Shamsi, *Selected Poems*, C.U.P., 1952, first edn. 1898

Tillich, Paul, *The Courage To Be*, Yale University Press, 1977

Underhill, Evelyn, *Practical Mysticism for Normal People*, Dent, 1914

Weatherhead, Leslie, *Wounded Spirits*, Hodder, 1962

For information on all books written by Peter Spink, contact: The Omega Order, Winford Manor, Winford, Avon BS18 8DW. Tel: 01275 472262, fax: 01275 472065.

Index

ABOUT THE AUTHOR

Canon Peter Spink was for five years a missionary working in the villages of Northern India. Returning to England he was ordained as an Anglican priest. His first parish was a new housing estate in the Midlands. From there he moved to become successively Chaplain to the British Embassies in Bonn, Vienna, Prague and Budapest. For nine years he worked on the staff of Coventry Cathedral of which he is a Canon. From 1977 to 1980 he was Warden of the Burrswood Home of Healing. He is the Founder of the Omega Order, a modern Ecumenical Religious Community which has its Headquarters at Winford Manor, Winford, Avon and a rapidly expanding worldwide teaching ministry.

THE OMEGA ORDER

The Order's teaching ministry is that of bringing people to the threshold of their own minds. It cuts across any form of indoctrination. The how of learning and the how of teaching are the cornerstones of its work. It has no doctrines of its own but seeks through the disciplines of contemplative awareness to penetrate the essence of all doctrine. Its point of beginning is the Christian religion and its perspective upon life relates to the words of Jesus 'I am the Alpha and the Omega, the first and the last . . .'

Piatkus Books

If you have enjoyed reading this book, you may be interested in other titles published by Piatkus. These include:

Care of the Soul: How to add depth and meaning to your everyday life Thomas Moore

Full Catastrophe Living: How to cope with stress, pain and illness using mindfulness meditation Jon Kabat-Zinn

Handbook for the Soul: A collection of writings from over 30 celebrated spiritual writers Richard Clarkson and Benjamin Shields (editors)

Hymns to an Unknown God: Awakening the spirit in everyday life Sam Keen

Lao Tzu's Tao Te Ching Timothy Freke

Meditation for Every Day: Includes over 100 inspiring meditations for busy people Bill Anderton

Mindfulness Meditation for Everyday Life Jon Kabat-Zinn

Rituals for Everyday Living: Special ways of marking important events in your life Lorna St Aubyn

The River of Life: A guide to your spiritual journey Ruth White

Teach Yourself to Meditate: Over 20 simple exercises for peace, health and clarity of mind Eric Harrison

The Three Minute Meditator: 30 simple ways to relax and unwind David Harp with Nina Feldman

Toward A Meaningful Life: The wisdom of the Rebbe Menachem Mendel Schneersohn Simon Jacobson (editor)

For a free brochure with information on our full range of titles, please write to:

Piatkus Books
Freepost 7 (WD 4505)
London W1E 4EZ

PIATKUS